PROPHECY
IN ACTION

There's a new wind blowing

PROPHECY IN ACTION

Father Jim Ferry and Dan Malachuk
as told to Howard and Beulah Earl

LOGOS INTERNATIONAL
PLAINFIELD, NEW JERSEY

Scripture is taken from the King James Version unless otherwise noted as NAB (New American Bible), RSV (Revised Standard Version), and TEV (Today's English Version).

PROPHECY IN ACTION
Copyright © 1978 by Logos International
All rights reserved
Printed in the United States of America
Library of Congress Catalog Card Number: 78-70749
International Standard Book Number: 0-88270-295-5 (hardcover)
0-88270-297-1 (paper)
Logos International, Plainfield, New Jersey 07060

THE AUTHORS

FATHER JIM FERRY   DAN MALACHUK

Dan Malachuk is president of Logos International Fellowship, Inc., a Christian publishing ministry which he and his wife, Viola, founded.

Father Jim Ferry is pastor of St. Antoninus Parish in inner-city Newark, and director of the People of HOPE, a large Catholic charismatic community based in northern New Jersey.

Dan and Father Ferry were co-chairmen of Jesus 78.

The Earls are a husband and wife writing team. Howard Earl, senior editor of *Logos Journal*, is a former radio and television commentator and writer and also served on the editorial staffs of several daily newspapers and national magazines. Beulah Earl, former columnist for the *Chicago Tribune* and radio and television scriptwriter, has worked with her husband on the editing and writing of several books and magazine articles.

Table of Contents

PROPHECY
IN ACTION

CHAPTER 1

A Fulfillment

Saturday, May 13, 1978, the day before Pentecost Sunday, dawned gray and cold with a threat of rain and a strong wind adding to the chill factor. Despite the dismal outlook, by seven-thirty that morning, roads leading to the home stadium of the National Football League's Giants and the Cosmos soccer team in the Meadowlands Sports Complex in East Rutherford, New Jersey were crowded with motor vehicles of every description. They were carrying Christians of many historic backgrounds—Catholic, Protestant-Evangelical, Messianic—and many non-believers coming as guests of the believers. They were hurrying to the Jesus 78 Rally.

By nine o'clock, when the official program began, at least 50,000 had arrived in the stadium and by mid-afternoon the attendance had numbered more than 60,000 to make the rally the greatest grass-roots interfaith gathering of Christians, sponsored by Catholics and Protestants, in the history of the United States and undoubtedly the world.

PROPHECY IN ACTION

There had been interfaith charismatic rallies at Notre Dame; in Kansas City, Missouri; Atlantic City, New Jersey and elsewhere but none to equal in numbers this one with its major purpose to promote unity in the Body of Jesus Christ and proclaim "Jesus is Lord."

What was the magnetism to attract such a crowd? What were the ingredients to bring together so many? And especially on a day that weather-wise promised only cold, high winds and rain? Registrations had been made for more than 60,000 to attend and rally sponsors estimated the attendance would have exceeded 70,000 had the weather been more favorable.

One might have credited the big name speakers as the main attraction. Ruth Carter Stapleton, Father Michael Scanlan, Jim Bakker, Andrae Crouch, and Father John Bertolucci assured strong appeal to charismatic Christians. But all attending were not charismatics.

The two visionaries of the Jesus 78 Rally—Father Jim Ferry, director of the People of HOPE, a Catholic charismatic community in Convent Station, New Jersey and Dan Malachuk, president of Logos International Fellowship, Inc., publishers of inspirational books and *Logos Journal*, a bimonthly charismatic magazine, in Plainfield, New Jersey—credited the one whose name was honored that day, Jesus Christ, and the purpose of the rally—to promote unity in the Body of Christ—as the magnetic attractions.

Considering the doctrinal differences in the Body of Christ, some might well have posed the question: "Can there be such a rally?" Amos 3:3 asks, "Can two walk together, except they be agreed?" There is supportive

A Fulfillment

Scripture to prove that they can. Ephesians 5:2 states, "And walk in love, as Christ also hath loved us and hath given himself for us."

Agreeing and walking in love is in accord with John 13:34, 35: "A new commandment I give unto you, That ye love one another; as I have loved you. . . . By this shall all men know that ye are my disciples, if ye have love one to another." We are reminded in Romans 3:23 that Christ died for all. "For all have sinned, and come short of the glory of God."

Father Ferry and Dan Malachuk point out that applying the quoted Scriptures and coming together in love and praise to God is the first step in the erasing of doctrinal differences—erasing them through the unity of the Holy Spirit, revealing the light and truth of God's Word.

Mindful of the above Scriptures, it was not happenstance or a casual agreement between two men to promote an interfaith rally that brought the idea to fruition. It was spawned by still further prophecies at previous charismatic conferences; prophecies which emphasized Christ's desire that those in His Body be brought together in unity of love and praise—not divided in doctrine, but one in the Holy Spirit. Unity does not mean union.

At the 1977 Conference on Charismatic Renewal in the Christian Churches, July 20-24, Kansas City, Missouri, Brick Bradford, of the Presbyterian Charismatic Communion, said that it was very possible that the Holy Spirit is preparing a renewal of the church in our time. Then he spoke some prophetic words when he said, "We

3

fully realize that the Lord has called us to be one, just as He and the Father are one. We honestly pray that we shall not be guilty of further fragmenting the Body of Christ. Therefore, we are endeavoring to contain some of the present-day Pentecost in existing structures, knowing very well that the Lord is quite capable of removing or changing those structures at His appointed time and in His own sovereign ways."

Then there was the prophecy given by Ralph Martin of the Word of God community, Ann Arbor, Michigan. In substance, the prophecy was, "The Body of my Son is broken. . . . Mourn and weep, for the Body of my Son is broken. . . . I am going to restore my people and reunite them. I am going to restore my people to the glory that is mine, so that the world might know that I am God and King and that I have come to redeem and save this earth. . . ."

These prophecies touched Father Ferry who, in addition to his directorship of the People of HOPE is administrator of the inner-city parish of St. Antoninus Roman Catholic Church in Newark, New Jersey. A few months after the conference in Kansas City, Father Ferry attended the Northeastern Catholic Regional Conference of Charismatics in Atlantic City, New Jersey. There additional prophecies on the unity of the Body of Christ were spoken.

At that conference were Dan Malachuk and his wife, Viola. The prophecies stirred in Dan a desire to become an instrument in bringing into reality the unity of the Body of Christ. It wasn't the first time Dan had heard this call for unity. It had been voiced in a conference he attended in

A Fulfillment

Lausanne, Switzerland, sponsored by Logos in July, 1977 and also an interfaith, multiracial conference in South Africa, co-sponsored by Logos. Now walking along Atlantic City's boardwalk he suddenly felt the Lord speaking to him directly and instructing him to take action. He wondered what and how.

Earlier Dan and Viola were seated near the front in an area assigned them as guests of the Atlantic City conference. Shortly before the celebration of the Eucharist, the priest pointed out the little message in the program which stated that, because of doctrinal differences, Protestants could not participate in a Roman Catholic Communion service. Dan and Viola merely stood while row after row of people filed by them to receive Communion.

"I stood there and wept," Viola related later. "I felt a rejection I had never experienced before. I felt as though these, my brethren, had judged me to be unworthy, not part of the Body of Christ—our Lord. It was a terrible feeling.

"As I stood there weeping, the Lord seemed to say to me, 'I too was rejected.' "

Viola shared her thoughts with Dan and asked, "How can we speak of unity when we can't even take Communion together?"

"But, dear," Dan remonstrated, "doctrines and traditions are not broken down overnight. We must wait for God's timing. He has His own ways which are above our ways and beyond our understanding. The walls will be broken down."

After his attempt to console Viola, Dan continued his

5

stroll along the boardwalk and suddenly came upon Father Ferry. "Jim," he said, as if directed by the Holy Spirit, "I believe it's time for you to consider including a broader number of Christians to participate in this type of conference."

Father Ferry spoke of the strong conviction he had for a closer unity as a result of the prophecies at Kansas City. Dan spoke of his conviction as a result of the prophecies he had heard at various conferences in charismatic circles. So as the two men strolled along with an ocean breeze blowing in upon them, Dan suggested, "Logos International will be pleased to cooperate in any way possible to bring unity and reconciliation among Christians."

Jim replied, "But we can't do this as a Catholic conference. We must open it up to all Christians."

There on the boardwalk the two men began to make plans for a giant interfaith charismatic rally. Father Ferry explained that he had driven by Giants' Stadium in the Meadowlands Sports Complex many times and thought how wonderful it would be if the stadium could be filled with Christians glorifying the name of the Lord.

"It would be a gigantic task for two men to attempt," he told Dan and then added, "but all things are possible with God."

Dan remembered those much-quoted words of Alfred, Lord Tennyson, "More things are wrought by prayer than this world dreams of."

So the initial phase of the Jesus 78 Rally moved from an idea into the planning stages. Meanwhile, in another part of the world the Holy Spirit was giving a message to Dr.

A Fulfillment

Vinson Synan, General Secretary of the Pentecostal Holiness Church. The similarity of the program envisioned by Dan and Father Ferry and the message received by Dr. Synan boggles the mind unless one accepts how the Holy Spirit communicates with God's children.

The message received by Dr. Synan came in an outline of ten suggestions or proposals for a Pentecost Day. The miracle of this is that Father Ferry and Dan were making plans for a rally to celebrate the Day of Pentecost the Saturday before Pentecost Sunday, and a thousand miles away the Holy Spirit was speaking to Dr. Synan, who recorded them and mailed the proposals to Leo Cardinal Joseph Suenens, Roman Catholic Primate of Belgium. The proposals were:

1. An around-the-world Pentecost Sunday be designated as a day for ecumenical celebration by people of all churches. That this be a "birthday celebration" for the birthday of the Church in which the coming of the Holy Spirit is recalled and emphasized.

2. That the ecumenical week in January has not had the impact that was desired, and that Pentecost Sunday is easier to remember and plan for. It is one of the three great feast days of the Church and should rank with Christmas and Easter as an important celebration for Christian people.

3. That the celebration be held in the afternoon or evening so that the people could attend their own services in the morning and come together in a central place later in the day. There would be no Eucharist in the celebration, thus avoiding the problems connected with

7

intercommunion.

(Note how proposal 3 followed the plan of Jesus 78 Rally. Instead of being held in the afternoon or evening of Pentecost Sunday so the people could attend their own churches in the morning, the rally was held the day preceding Pentecost so those of all denominations and historic church backgrounds could attend without missing their Pentecost Sunday services and take communion.)

4. The celebration would be local city-wide efforts and not national or provincial in scope. Costs would thus be minimized—no hotel or restaurant costs and so forth. The only cost might be for renting a large auditorium which could accommodate the crowds. Local speakers would be used as much as possible.

(Note again the similarity between the Jesus 78 Rally and the proposals in number 4. There was no plan to make the rally nationwide. A stadium was rented. The people came from areas sufficiently nearby to make any overnight lodging unnecessary.)

5. The leadership in each city would consist of responsible charismatic and pentecostal priests, pastors and prayer group leaders. Non-charismatic leadership and participation would be welcomed, but the tone and style would be charismatic.

(Here again the proposal followed almost exactly the way the Jesus 78 Rally was carried out.)

6. As much as possible, the celebration would be an attempt to carry to the local, grass-roots level, the joy and power of the Charismatic Conference on Renewal in the Christian Churches which convened in Kansas City, Missouri in July, 1977. The type of planning committee

A Fulfillment

and program might well be patterned after the Kansas City model.

(Jesus 78 was carried to the grass-roots level and did to a certain degree pattern after the Kansas City Charismatic Conference on Renewal. But there were certain limitations on a one-day rally as compared to the Kansas City four-day conference.)

7. Pentecost Day celebrations would arise from the common people of the cities of the world. Of course effective celebration would not occur where local vision and leadership were not adequate. But where possible, great Pentecost Sunday celebrations would create the interest and enthusiasm for others in neighboring cities. In time the whole Christian world could be enriched annually as believers from all denominations gathered on Pentecost Sunday to proclaim that "Jesus is Lord" in the power of the Holy Spirit.

(Again the proposal received by Dr. Synan boggles the mind when compared to the thinking of Dan and Father Ferry. Following the success of the Jesus 78 Rally, they immediately set in motion plans to hold Jesus 79 rallies in at least 15 other cities next June 2, the day preceding Pentecost.)

8. These celebrations would be an opportunity to share a common witness to the Church and the world about the outpouring of the Holy Spirit "upon all flesh" in these days. The infectious joy and power of the Holy Spirit would then flow back into the churches and bless them.

9. Coming from these celebrations would be a new level of unity between the Christian churches in response to Jesus' prayer, "That they all may be one, even as my

Father and I are one." The unity of the Spirit must be demonstrated before any kind of structural unity can be contemplated. Being together at one time and one place in unity (as in the upper room) would go far to heal the divisions which have fractured the Body of Christ for centuries. This witness to Christian unity would be one of the prime fruits of such a celebration.

10. The cause of evangelism would be strengthened from such united witnesses occurring around the world. Our unity in Christ through the Holy Spirit would be a sign to the non-Christian world "that they might believe."

Dr. Synan's prophecy from the Holy Spirit may have been a spiritual follow-up of the conference in Kansas City which he attended. Asked to reflect on what that conference would mean for the charismatic renewal and for the churches, Dr. Synan told *New Covenant* magazine, "The conference was not just a call for unity. It was a demonstration of the unity the Lord has already given. . . . I think the conference will confront religious leaders who are not in the charismatic renewal. The message of Kansas City is that the charismatic renewal is the most vibrant, powerful force in Christendom today, and that this great force is not going to be fragmented but is going to move in the same direction."

Dr. Synan was overwhelmed when he learned that the prophecy given to him by the Holy Spirit in October, 1977 was fulfilled by the Jesus 78 Rally. He knew nothing about the plans for the rally when he received the message, and neither did Dan and Father Ferry know he had received the proposals and sent a copy to Cardinal Suenens. Neither did the two men realize the gigantic task which

A Fulfillment

lay ahead as they set about laying plans for the rally.
They had caught a vision and implementing it meant
making the arrangements to rent Giants' Stadium,
engaging speakers well known in charismatic circles,
arranging for music, registrations, publicity and making
certain the program was well balanced between
Protestant and Catholic speakers. It was a task they could
not handle alone, so a planning committee was named.
Serving on that committee were Dan, Al Malachuk,
brother of Dan, Bob Armbruster, Jane Henry from Logos
and Father Ferry, Bob Gallic, Father Bob Brennan,
Sister Julia Jamink, S.C., Betty McElhill and Louise
Jacobsen from the People of HOPE.

To Al Malachuk and Bob Gallic went the task of
negotiating for the rental of Giants' Stadium and setting
up the "One in the Spirit" nights in various locations in
states from where it was hoped attendance would be
drawn for the rally. Bob Armbruster was named to head
up the publicity for the rally with help from Father Bob
Brennan. Both the People of HOPE and Logos would
handle registrations. The immediate and vital task was to
select the featured speakers and contact them to
determine if they would be available.

The planning committee decided on four featured
speakers, two Catholic and two Protestant, to balance the
program. In addition, it was decided to contact the agent
of Andrae Crouch to engage him for special music and his
testimony. The Protestants were Ruth Carter Stapleton,
well-known evangelist with a healing ministry, author of
The Gift of Inner Healing and *The Experience of Inner
Healing* and sister of President Jimmy Carter; and Jim

Bakker, host and founder of the Christian television talk show "PTL Club" which can mean either "Praise The Lord" or "People That Love." He also is author of *Move That Mountain!* and *The Big Three Mountain-Movers.*

The Catholic speakers selected were Father John P. Bertolucci, called by some the "Catholic Billy Graham," pastor of St. Joseph's Roman Catholic Parish in Little Falls, New York and former vice chancellor of the Albany, New York diocese; and Father Michael Scanlan, a Franciscan priest, president of the College of Steubenville in Ohio and immediate past chairman of the Catholic Charismatic Renewal in the United States and author of *The Power in Penance, Inner Healing* and *And Their Eyes Were Opened.*

Andrae Crouch was chosen because of his widespread popularity as a soul gospel singer with special talent for reaching youth. He has been the recipient of pop music's highest honor, the Grammy Award, and in 1977 he and his "Disciples" received the Dove Award, given to the top soul gospel group of the year.

Thus was the machinery set in motion for what would become the greatest Catholic-Protestant ecumenical gathering in history.

CHAPTER 2

Planning and Preparation

Once the decision was made to go forward with plans to hold Jesus 78 in Giants' Stadium, praying and planning became vital factors. Al Malachuk and Bob Gallic were named to coordinate the overall activities at Giants' Stadium. They met early in December with John Krumpe, Executive Director of the New Jersey Sports and Exposition Authority, and Bill Barnhill, Supervisor of Stadium Operations, to review the contract for the rental of the stadium on May 13 and discuss the various activities and duties connected with parking facilities, ushering, concessions and a variety of details.

Al and Bob were pleasantly surprised in the lobby of the building housing the offices of the Meadowlands Sports Complex. They were waiting for their appointment with Krumpe and Barnhill when three of the telephone operators at the switchboard began asking questions concerning Jesus 78. They wanted to know what it was all about.

One operator said she had a boyfriend who attended an

Assembly of God church in the area and he told her that he had a born-again experience. She asked, "Exactly what is a born-again experience? What did he mean?" Al and Bob explained to her the plan of salvation. The other operators seemed to be listening when not occupied at the switchboard. There were other opportunities to witness since many of the employees at the stadium said they had never worked with a group such as the one sponsoring Jesus 78. "They were most cooperative," Al said.

Several of the Pinkerton security officers were born-again believers. When they heard they were going to be assigned to the Jesus 78 Rally they expressed delight because they would be a part of the overall program. One of them exclaimed, "Praise the Lord!"

Al said, "It seemed as though the Lord kept opening doors and opportunities so that we might be able to continue as strong witnesses wherever we made contact in the planning stages. We could feel the power of prayer and knew that many Protestant and Catholic prayer groups were praying for the Lord to make the rally a great day for the glory of Jesus Christ."

The Lord impressed upon publisher Dan Malachuk that it would be helpful to those attending the rally to develop the May/June issue of *Logos Journal* into a souvenir issue of Jesus 78. He and the editorial staff discussed the type of editorial content most appropriate for such an issue and decided upon the format. Al and Bob, upon receiving this news, made plans for disbursement of the souvenir issue at the rally. Since the Stevens Concession organization normally handled the sales of such items they took over the *Journal* sales.

Al found it interesting comparing how the Stevens personnel handled the sale of the *Journal* with the sales of programs at a Cosmos soccer or Giants football game. There was something almost reverent in the way they exhorted the people, "Read all about Jesus 78 and who the speakers are for the day." At a soccer or football game they usually bellowed, "Get your program and know who the players are."

"All in all," Al said, "the cooperation by the Sports Authority personnel was excellent from the ticket takers to the security guards who assisted our people and ushers in directing people to the areas where the book and record tables were set up on each of the three levels. Over 14,000 books and records were sold during the day. The majority of the books were published by Logos, Servant, Dimension, Ave Maria and Word.

Another facet of the overall plans for making the Jesus 78 Rally as widely publicized as possible involved "One in the Spirit" nights.

The planning committee started laying the groundwork for a general meeting the evening of December 16 at Xavier Center in Convent Station. Invited were Christian leaders from all groups and denominations. The format for the evening included messages from a Catholic and a Protestant leader and a lay witness. Letters were written to pastors, officers of the Full Gospel Business Men's Fellowship and Women's Aglow chapters and church leaders, inviting them to attend. Flyers (handbills) were printed announcing the meeting and giving a few of the particulars. Volunteers placed the flyers in key public places in addition to churches and business establishments.

Father Joseph Orsini, Assistant Director of the Charismatic Renewal for the Diocese of Camden, New Jersey and Campus Minister at Rutgers University, was the Catholic speaker for the evening. He is also author of the following Logos books: *Hear My Confession, The Anvil, The Cost in Pentecost* and *Papa Bear's Favorite Italian Dishes*. The Protestant speaker was the Reverend David Hannon, pastor of the First Christian Assembly in Plainfield, New Jersey. Speaking as a lay witness, Gary Cuozzo, former quarterback of the Baltimore Colts and Minnesota Vikings, gave his testimony. People of HOPE invited their whole community and prayer fellowship.

Christian leaders who the committee believed could be instrumental in organizing future "One in the Spirit" meetings, were invited to attend a fellowship dinner preceding the meeting. It was explained to them how they could initiate meetings in their areas, based on the committee's experience in arranging the first one. The committee offered to assist others in their "One in the Spirit" meetings by printing flyers, helping to arrange for speakers, putting leaders in touch with leaders of other faiths in their own areas and providing general encouragement.

An offering was taken to help defray expenses. It was suggested that this be done at future meetings to make them as self-supporting as possible.

The initial gathering at Convent Station was attended by about 800 people, forty of whom were leaders who were considering holding "One in the Spirit" meetings in their areas. Many returned home, got on the telephone with their Catholic and Protestant counterparts. They met with each other, drew more friends into their circles, prayed together and sought the Lord's healing and direction. Plans for additional meetings began to emerge. There were occasional disagreements but God laid his blanket of love over them as they went to prayer to solve their differences.

"God was at work healing," Al Malachuk explained. "And He healed His broken Body in all the preliminary meetings."

Many locations in New Jersey, New York, Connecticut, Rhode Island and Pennsylvania were the site of "One in the Spirit" meetings. Dan and Al Malachuk, Father Ferry and Bob Gallic were called upon to speak at many of the meetings. They traveled many miles at times to fulfill the requests. The meetings were so spiritually uplifting that some people attended four or five of them. Often referred to as nights of preparation because they focused on the upcoming Jesus 78 Rally, some thirty were held between the first one at Convent Station and the final one preceding the rally.

At each meeting, the audience was told all about Jesus 78. Registrations were received for people who wanted to attend the rally in groups of ten and single parties. Posters and bumper stickers were distributed and flyers given out in bulk numbers so that they could be distributed in churches and prayer groups. "It was evident from the conversations following a "One in the Spirit" meeting," said Al, "that people were blessed of

17

the Lord as they came together, unmindful of their denominational labels. They worshiped Him with uncluttered minds in simple love and that was most important of all."

Logos provided art work, when needed, and printing services for the "One in the Spirit" flyers. Local leaders brought their information to Logos and the print shop produced 5,000 to 15,000 copies of the flyers to advertise a meeting. Also printed by Logos were 500,000 Jesus 78 flyers, 50,000 bumper stickers, bookmarks and letters.

Approximately every two weeks the People of HOPE sent a newsletter to all "One in the Spirit" leaders, keeping them informed about the latest plans for Jesus 78 and to advise where meetings were being held. The newsletter carried timely suggestions and served to make all the subleaders and "One in the Spirit" people feel that they were a part of the team. It also kept the goal ever upon the leaders' minds—"get the people to Giants' Stadium on May 13."

The format of the meetings changed slightly about two months after the December 16 meeting. Many of the groups showed the film *Jesus is Lord*, a documentary on the Kansas City Charismatic Conference in July, 1977. The film proved so exciting and so well done that it greatly increased interest to attend the Jesus 78 Rally. So well was it received that it was decided to suggest that it be included as a part of each meeting. However, it was found when the film was used the speakers should be limited to two so the meeting would not run over two hours which seemed to be the proper time limit.

"At a 'One in the Spirit' meeting in a Presbyterian

church in Westfield, New Jersey," explained Al
Malachuck, "the people became so totally caught up in the
28-minute film that they clapped their hands and sang
with it."

In a Jesus 78 Update Bulletin, dated February 8, 1978,
mailed by the People of HOPE, the dates of upcoming
"One in the Spirit" nights were listed together with the
location and the speakers. Suggestions for the use of
flyers also were included along with a basic outline for the
meetings. The format called for opening the meeting with
praise, singing and prayer for fifteen minutes, then the
Kansas City film *Jesus is Lord*, followed by the first
speaker. After the message came a praise break, then the
second speaker, followed by praise, announcements,
offering and the final prayer. The bulletin explained how
the Kansas City film could be obtained and the telephone
number and person to contact for additional information.
The suggested format, of course, could be altered.

In a special communication over the signature of Father
Jim Ferry and Dan Malachuk, mailed just nineteen days
before the Jesus 78 Rally, a special request was made.
The announcement read in part: "The nine days preceding
Pentecost are going to be a special time of prayer and
fasting for the members of the People of HOPE and of
Logos International Fellowship. We feel a special
anointing on the enclosed pamphlet, 'Nine Days of Prayer
to the Holy Spirit.' At the residential HOPE centers and
at the Logos offices the prayer will be said at noon from
May 5 to May 12. We invite you to join us at one of these
locations . . . or to gather at a church or other place more
convenient for your group . . . or to say the prayer

privately. Our prayer is 'That all may be one' " (John 17:21).

The communication further stated that the "One in the Spirit" nights had planted seeds of unity which needed watering. People were encouraged to continue praying and being instruments of the Lord in organizing continuing "One in the Spirit" gatherings in their areas because Jesus 78 "is just the beginning."

At Logos many members of the office staff volunteered their time willingly to phone leaders of prayer groups and churches to encourage them to hold "One in the Spirit" meetings in their areas.

Summing up the part he played in the planning and preparations for Jesus 78, Al Malachuk said, "The most delightful experience I had was assisting in the organization of the "One in the Spirit" nights. Many beautiful people were so anxious to become involved, listening attentively to what was required to be done to make the night successful.

"It was a privilege to visit many of the prayer groups and churches and encourage the people to become involved prior to the "One in the Spirit" nights that were set up in the greater New York area.

"Another exhilarating moment was when we met with representatives of the Council of Churches of the City of New York. They listened to our plans and purposes for Jesus 78 in the Meadowlands and the Board of Directors gave their wholehearted support."

CHAPTER 3

Alerting the Public

Once Father Jim Ferry and Dan Malachuk made their decision to hold the Jesus 78 Rally and arrangements were completed for rental of Giants' Stadium, the next move was to start a publicity campaign. Both men were sufficiently schooled in promotion to realize that a rally such as they envisioned would need concentrated promotion and much prayer. They immediately set in motion a crash promotion program, headed by former newspaperman Bob Armbruster of the *Logos Journal* editorial staff. Bob had been on the editorial staffs of the Bergen *Record* in New Jersey, the Paulist Press and the Christian biweekly newspaper, the *National Courier*. He knew his way around in newspaper circles which promised to be a valuable asset. He would quickly learn the approach necessary to interest the television and radio newspeople.

The first thing an experienced newsperson looks for in a publicity release is an attention-grabber to interest the readers. News editor Ed Grant of the Catholic

Archdiocese of Newark's *Advocate* used a quote by Father Ferry who had quipped, "We might even be able to work a miracle and get the Giants an offense." The *Advocate* was the first newspaper to publish a story on the Jesus 78 Rally.

Another newspaper to carry an early story was a large suburban one in Bergen County, New Jersey, *The Record*, where Armbruster actually began his journalistic career. The newspaper's religion editor, Wilma Supik, headlined her story, "Charismatics Pray Where Giants Play," a unique attention-getter.

The *Washington Star* was another early bird on the Jesus 78 bandwagon. Religion editor Bill Willoughby handled the news release so adeptly that Armbruster sent copies of the story to many daily and weekly newspapers in the hopes that the editors would be impressed by the *Star* carrying an article on the event and do likewise. How many were impressed is unknown but the tempo of the publicity carried by newspapers increased.

An additional helping hand came from Roger Conant and Bob Importico, two young copy editors on the Newark *Star-Ledger*, New Jersey's largest daily newspaper. Armbruster was told that they were interested in the charismatic renewal. They were mailed the initial press releases and close contact was maintained with them. Conant finally indicated that he and Importico would be interested in doing a feature piece that went beyond the press releases. An interview was set for them with Father Ferry, Dan Malachuk and Dan's brother, Al, who was handling registrations for Jesus 78 at Logos, making arrangements for the locations of the "One in the

Spirit" nights and maintaining an ecumenical balance of leaders for the meetings.

Commenting on the interview and subsequent story, Armbruster said, "Monica Maske, the *Star-Ledger*'s religion editor, rewrote the interview for publication in the Sunday paper. It was given good space with photos of Father Ferry, Dan Malachuk and Ruth Carter Stapleton. Its publication was extremely helpful in giving people in the New Jersey area a well-rounded idea of the upcoming Jesus 78 Rally."

The second press release in March headlined the fact that Ruth Carter Stapleton would speak. The release was sent to hundreds of daily and weekly newspapers in New Jersey, New York, Pennsylvania and Connecticut, the states from which the most people would be attracted to the rally. Along with the release went a photo of Mrs. Stapleton.

Armbruster, in commenting on the publicity techniques, said, "Personal notes were sent with the press releases to religion editors of many of the daily papers. Newspersons are always more interested in mail that is personally addressed. Phone calls were made to quite a few of the newspapers to learn the names of their religion editors. Where practical the press releases were personalized. For example, the release sent to the *Jersey Journal* in Jersey City noted that Father Ferry was a native of Bayonne, he had attended high school and college in Jersey City and served at a parish in the area covered by the *Journal.*"

The list of newspapers giving space and support to publicizing the rally were many. The Catholic diocesan newspapers—particularly *The Advocate* of Newark, *The Beacon* of Paterson and *The Long Island Catholic*—were most helpful. Liz O'Connor of *The Long Island Catholic* drove to New Jersey to interview Father Ferry for a major story on The People of HOPE as well as Jesus 78. Father Ferry commented later that Liz's story was one of the best ever done on The People of HOPE.

Wilma Supik, mentioned earlier, showed a strong interest from the day the rally was announced. She visited both HOPE and Logos International Fellowship in Plainfield for a major feature story on born-again Christians. The article appeared in *The Record*'s life style section the Sunday before the rally. Marcia Leahy, religion editor of the *Asbury Park Press*, displayed consistent interest and did a feature story on a "One in the Spirit" night. Another religion editor, Nancy Taylor of the *Morristown Daily Record*, kept in close touch with developments preceding the rally. Chris Satullo also devoted considerable news space to the rally in the *Easton Express* in Pennsylvania.

"Another avenue of publicity opened to us," comments Armbruster, "was a number of charismatic newsletters. *The Good News Letter* for the charismatic renewal in Virginia, the newsletters for the charismatic renewal in the Archdiocese of Newark and the Dioceses of Trenton and Rockville Centre and others gave good advance coverage. *Alternatives*, a Christian magazine for the New York metropolitan area, gave the rally coverage."

Another facet not overlooked by Armbruster was the New Jersey chapter of the Society of Professional Journalists. He attended meetings of the chapter to develop more media contacts. Lending advice and support was Father Michael Russo of the Newark archdiocese communications office. Most helpful also were Les Unger and Mike Graime of the Meadowlands public relations staff, especially in planning for the news media coverage on the day of the rally.

In the final days preceding Jesus 78, interest among the press people intensified. One newspaper in particular, which had ignored all press releases, evidently was suddenly awakened to the enormity of the event through stories appearing in many of the other publications and carried an article. On the Sunday before the rally, stories appeared in *The Record* of Bergen County, Newark's *Star-Ledger* and the New Jersey editions of the New York *Daily News* and *The New York Times.* Someone called this "a grand slam."

Television and radio played an important role in publicizing the rally. Father Bob Brennan of The People of HOPE and Joe Chomyn of the Community of God's Love in Rutherford were helpful in the television effort. Dick Hirsch of the United States Catholic Conference staff proved instrumental in urging the religious affairs department of CBS, headed by vice president Pamela Ilott, to do a 28-minute special on Jesus 78. The program, produced by Joe Clement, appeared on CBS affiliates throughout the country the second Sunday after the rally.

Representatives of The People of HOPE and Logos International appeared on a number of radio programs and a couple of cable television shows. Betty McElhill of HOPE and Armbruster were on the Acts 29 radio program in Philadelphia from midnight to 1:30 A.M. on a

PROPHECY IN ACTION

Sunday morning. Many of the charismatics in Philadelphia and the surrounding area listen to this program, so it was considered quite successful in building interest for the rally. (Acts 29 has moved since to a better time slot.) There were interviews on a radio station in Elizabeth and on WERA in Plainfield. Father Brennan and Armbruster appeared on a cable television program telecast in Port Jervis, New York.

No one really knew what to expect the day of the rally regarding the exact number of reporters to be accommodated in the press room of Giants' Stadium. Provision had been made to serve coffee and a light lunch. Some typewriters had been rented. As it turned out, the metropolitan news media, encompassing an area of New York, New Jersey and Pennsylvania, were well represented. More bona-fide reporters showed than had come to any of the previous charismatic conferences in the area. The fruit of the publicity effort, extending over several weeks, was reflected in the number of stories on the rally reported by the news media.

The New York Times, The Record of Bergen County, Newark's *Star-Ledger, Asbury Park Press, Morristown Daily Record, Hudson Dispatch, Passaic Herald News* and *Peekskill Evening Star* carried major stories on Jesus 78. The *Washington Star* gave very good space to wire service photos. The *Atlanta Journal* and *Constitution* and other papers published the *New York Times* wire service story. Particularly impressive was a front-page color photo in the *Morristown Daily Record* by Bruce Crawford. It featured a banner which proclaimed "Jesus is Lord."

Alerting the Public

The Advocate had its entire staff, under the direction of its executive director Jim Dulan and managing editor Joe Thomas, produce a special supplement on Jesus 78. Other Catholic papers giving coverage included the *Paterson Beacon*, *Camden Catholic Star Herald*, and the *Long Island Catholic*. *The Evangelist* of the Albany, New York diocese and the *Catholic Standard* of the Washington, D.C. archdiocese were among the Catholic newspapers giving space to the National Catholic News Service story.

The Acts 29 radio ministry arranged to have a significant portion of Jesus 78 transmitted to radio stations in Pennsylvania, southern New Jersey, Delaware, Maryland, Florida and Washington, D.C. WWDJ—located in Hackensack, New Jersey—also presented a major portion of the program in the afternoon. Don Lettieri of Acts 29, Joe Battaglia of WWDJ and Allen Dixon of WCTN in Maryland all manifested much interest in Jesus 78 from the time of its inception.

Television stations which presented spots (film clips) on the Saturday evening news, May 13, included CBS, NBC and ABC. Radio station WMTR in the Morristown area broadcast excerpts from the featured speakers' messages on Sunday mornings during July. The PTL television network presented a major segment of the Jesus 78 Rally some days after the event. And much farther away, a West German television station had a crew at the rally taping it for a future showing in West Germany.

News services which carried significant stories were

those of *The New York Times,* Associated Press, United Press International, National Catholic News Service and Religious News Service.

An indication of how well the sponsors of Jesus 78 publicized the event comes from PTL's Jim Bakker. When he learned that less than $500 had been spent on advertising, he had second thoughts about sending his television crew to the rally, and even attending himself as one of the featured speakers.

"I thought," Jim admitted later, "such a small amount spent on advertising! What if I go through the expense of sending my television crew with all the equipment from Charlotte, North Carolina to East Rutherford, New Jersey and there are only around 200 people there?"

One really couldn't fault Jim for having misgivings about an event on which so little had been spent for advertising. It was an astonished Jim Bakker who walked to the podium in Giants' Stadium and faced 60,000 cheering welcomers as he was introduced. No less surprised by the size of the crowd were some of the seasoned reporters covering the rally. New York *Daily News'* columnist John McLaughlin wrote, "I was unprepared for the fervor, serenity and friendliness of it all."

Distributed to members of the news media at the rally were press kits containing the program for the day, a feature story on the rally, biographies of the speakers and the chairman and co-chairman of the rally, definitions of charismatic terminology, a *Logos Journal* souvenir issue, People of HOPE *Newsletter* and an article on the Baptism in the Holy Spirit.

Alerting the Public

The well-planned and activated publicity campaign had borne fruit, but supplementing the publicity was the operation of the administrative office at Logos under the direction of Al Malachuk, assisted by his competent secretary Jane Henry. Letters were mailed to many Christian bookstores inviting them to accept admission registrations from their customers (at a ten percent commission) and display Jesus 78 Rally posters in their stores. Approximately seventy-five bookstores responded. A simple bookkeeping system was set up to record ticket consignments and registrations. Some bookstores recorded registrations for over five hundred tickets and some refused to take the ten percent commission. Many bookstores attracted new customers as a result of this service.

Other lay and professional people were given tickets on consignment to distribute for admission registrations in their churches, prayer groups, at Full Gospel Business Men's meetings, at Aglow meetings, at "One in the Spirit" nights and so forth.

"The consignment of tickets proved helpful," explained Jane Henry, "but many hours were spent on the phone calling bookstores and others, asking them to turn in the money or tickets. A deadline for consignment returns or payment was set for April 28 in order to give the committee a fairly accurate count of tickets out. Some 20,000 tickets were out on consignment at the deadline date, so it was of vital importance for us to know how many had been subscribed to. We didn't want to have more tickets subscribed for than the stadium could accommodate. Neither did we want to turn down ticket consignments if we hadn't oversubscribed."

It was a dilemma which was given over to the Lord in prayer, asking Him to see that everyone who wanted to attend the rally and who He wanted to come would be there. Meanwhile, to facilitate the disbursement of tickets during the last few weeks, special locations were set up, including bookstores, churches, and centers affiliated with the People of HOPE—no more than ten in all. All other tickets supposedly had been called in by this time so these special centers were supplied with several hundred tickets.

Up to the time these centers were established most of the tickets had been subscribed to by mail. Orders received were filled each day as they came in to Logos and HOPE with a record kept of the number of adult, youth and children's tickets ordered. In mailing out the tickets, a bumper sticker promoting Jesus 78, a Bible bookmark and a cover letter were included. Copies of all checks were made for the files and the original checks sent to the People of HOPE for banking.

Letters were sent to pastors of several denominations where their names were available, inviting them to attend the rally, offering them advertising literature for their churches and encouraging them to attend by offering two guest tickets to each pastor contacted.

Letters also were mailed to every mayor in New Jersey (almost 600), every state senator and assembly person offering them two free tickets and a seat in a special reserved section for dignitaries. Unfortunately, most of these dignitaries could not attend because they need at least three months' notice for scheduling purposes.

Alerting the Public

"Another job for our office," said Jane, "was to make name badges for all the official and staff workers and parking permits for cars. The last few days preceding the rally the telephone rang incessantly. Among other requests, some news people wanted private interviews with the speakers.

"Then there were phone calls from people seeking general information, such as when would Ruth Carter Stapleton speak, is there a chartered bus leaving for the stadium from a certain area, or how could tickets be ordered? Several wanted to sell merchandise at the stadium or distribute free literature. Some performing groups wanted permission to put on their acts during the rally."

The People of HOPE received a phone call from a man who said he was training some pigeons and he wanted to release them in the stadium during the Jesus 78 Rally. Father Ferry wanted to know if they really were well trained. He refused the offer fearing that a flock of pigeons over the stadium, if they hovered too long, might prove embarrassing to the many dignitaries out on the field.

Somehow all the questions were answered. All the chores were done, hopefully to the satisfaction of everyone. And one can truthfully report that a great sigh of relief emanated from the scores of workers when the curtain rang down on the final hour of the Jesus 78 Rally at Giants' Stadium.

CHAPTER 4

LIF: A Brief History

The normal individual would consider it incredible to turn from a profession which brought him financial success and enter a business venture about which he knew nothing. But Dan Malachuk is considered unusual by many for a variety of reasons. Foremost he places explicit trust in the Lord. When he feels the Lord's leading, he acts. That was no more emphatically demonstrated than in 1968.

President of a successful retail jewelry business, Dan also was involved with the Full Gospel Business Men's Fellowship, International (FGBMFI).

"I found myself in the 1960s heading up a series of charismatic seminars for the FGBMFI," explains Dan. "Things were moving along smoothly and, at forty-five, I was actually thinking quite seriously about an early retirement. But the Lord had other ideas."

The turnabout in Dan's contemplated plans began in 1965 when the FGBMFI scheduled an airlift to London, England. Dan was placed in charge of one of the plane loads of businessmen and their wives departing from

Idlewild (now Kennedy) Airport. Two significant developments occurred during that trip. Dan explains:

"In England I came across a series of revealing lectures on the snares of spiritualism written by a former spiritualist medium by the name of Raphael Gasson. The lectures, entitled *The Challenging Counterfeit*, gave an inside look at the dangers of spiritualism as well as an account of the author's deliverance from it, his conversion and new-birth experience as a follower of Jesus Christ. I was alerted by the Lord that interest in spiritualism and other occult religions would increase in the United States in coming years. As a means of combating it, I was impressed to secure the rights to the book in the United States."

Dan's message from the Lord was accurate and timely. Involvement in the occult did increase in the United States and is flourishing today, even being taught in some of our universities. *The Challenging Counterfeit* proved a helpful instrument in informing the public what really lies behind those religions.

The book was Dan's first venture into the publishing field. He recalls, "I returned home to central New Jersey, sent a copy of the manuscript to a printer and ordered 10,000 copies. I also arranged a royalty schedule with Raphael Gasson. When the books arrived from the printer, we began shipping them out from the rear of our jewelry store in Plainfield. Now I was a publisher."

The second major significant factor in Dan's entering the publishing business also occurred while he was in England with the FGBMFI. He met Nicky Cruz, former gang warlord in New York City and a spiritual hero in

David Wilkerson's *The Cross and the Switchblade*.
Several months later Nicky called Dan for assistance in
finding a writer for his story, *Run Baby Run*. Through an
introduction provided by John Sherrill, then an editor
with *Guideposts* magazine, Dan and his wife, Viola,
partners in the publishing venture, met Jamie
Buckingham who was attending a *Guideposts'* Writers
Institute in New York. Less than a year after that first
meeting with Buckingham *Run Baby Run* was published.
John and Tib Sherrill kindly assisted them as editorial
advisors for *Run Baby Run*.

That same year, 1968, saw two other books come off the
printing presses: *The Grace and the Glory of God* by Ray
Jarman and Carmen Benson and *These Are Not Drunken
as Ye Suppose* by Dr. Howard Ervin. The Malachuks
were in the publishing business in earnest.

Announcement of the formation of Logos International
brought an unexpected but welcome response from two
Holy Spirit-filled friends. Art and Eleanor Duble went to
them and offered financial assistance. Subsequently the
Dubles organized Logos Tapes, a ministry which today
circulates thousands of teaching cassettes recorded by
prominent Christian Bible teachers.

"In those early days of our new venture," recalls Dan,
"we made do with what facilities came easily to hand. The
kitchen table in our home served as the editor's desk for a
while. As we began to add titles we established an
editorial office and order department in the basement of
our home where Viola began to do the editing. Through all
of this we were very conscious of God's help. He had to be
at our side because neither Viola nor I had any

background in publishing or any skills necessary in that field."

Dan still remembers one of the first times he met with a printer's representative. The representative began talking to Dan and Viola, using technical terms they had never heard. Finally, in desperation, Dan took a book from a nearby shelf and showed it to the man. "See this book," he said. "I want you to make a book to look like this one." Thus the first Logos book was on its way.

As word of the new Christian publishing venture spread, the number of incoming manuscripts from those seeking publication increased. Month by month the staff grew. Finally the store adjacent to the Plainfield jewelry store was remodeled into an office but even this became inadequate space. Buildings next to the jewelry store were either rented or purchased. Meanwhile an increasing number of books were arriving from the printer. It became a fast-multiplying game with more books selected for publication and greater numbers of books to be marketed.

In October of 1971 through a series of spiritual coincidences, the help of Joseph Mattson-Boze and Gerald Derstine, and the intervention of the Lord, Logos International stepped out in a new publication venture—*Logos Journal*. Since the name *Logos*, meaning "the Word," had been chosen as the name of the publishing company, it was thought appropriate that the new bimonthly magazine should be given the same name. Like the first book, the *Journal* came into being on the Malachuks' kitchen table.

The late Al West was called from Tampa, Florida to be

the magazine's editor. Donna, his wife, served as his secretary. Before additional help was engaged, Al was responsible for paste-up and layout as well as the selection of articles to be published. As the *Logos Journal* circulation increased, costs and salaries had to be met and the book division of Logos International subsidized the magazine.

"Viola and I had determined that any and all profits from our publishing ventures would be used for the ministry of the Word," Dan recalls. "This was a part of our life style when I was a jeweler and our practice has continued in a natural way throughout the years."

Another ministry was born as a result of publication of *Run Baby Run* and Merlin Carothers' *Prison to Praise*. Prisoners began to read these two bestsellers and started writing Logos, asking for more books and Bibles. Many heart-warming testimonies came from inmates whose lives had been changed by reading those books. The first personal answers to prisoners' letters were written by Pat Blackburn, a woman who, as a result of a severe attack of polio, has been confined for more than twenty years to a wheelchair and breathing machine. She's completely paralyzed except for the ability to use two fingers. Pat uses a tape recorder to answer prisoners' letters and several typists transcribe them.

Now over 500 pen pals are corresponding with more than 1,500 prisoners weekly through the Logos pen pal program. A group of housewives spend many hours each week writing personal letters of counsel and help to more than 800 prisoners. The prison ministry also has developed close contact with many chaplains throughout the United States prison system.

"Soon we began to realize there were other needs among the prisoners that Logos could meet," explains Dan. "So we founded a unique tabloid newspaper, *The Crack in the Wall*, a publication written by prisoners for prisoners. Today over 50,000 copies of the tabloid are being distributed free of charge in over 500 prisons in this country and overseas."

Originally the book division of Logos International was under Danmal, Inc., a profit corporation with a board of directors for spiritual and managerial guidance. Dan and Viola were the only stockholders. In 1977 they directed that the stock, ownership, copyrights and profits of Danmal, Inc., be transferred to the nonprofit, Christian ministry, Logos International Fellowship, Inc. A board of trustees directs the ministry's activities.

For many years Logos International, publisher of Christian books, sponsored all the ministries of Logos International Fellowship. However, as LIF's outreach expanded it became necessary to ask for assistance from concerned individuals. To date, 15,000 people who share LIF's vision have provided financial assistance for the ministries. Many have made tax-deductible contributions, while others have taken advantage of the opportunity for Christian financial involvement through special arrangements on a long-term basis.

Dan Malachuk explains that LIF's purposes are three-fold. The first is to communicate the gospel of Jesus Christ throughout the entire world by every means possible; the second, to make historic churches aware of

LIF: A Brief History

God's power; the third is to serve as a bridge to understanding and love among people of all nations and denominations in order to be part of the answer to Jesus Christ's prayer that His people would all be one in love and in spirit.

In October, 1975 the first national Christian newspaper, the *National Courier*, was published by LIF. Prior to its publication, in order to accommodate an enlarging staff, LIF purchased the building vacated by the *Courier-News* when it moved its headquarters out of Plainfield. The purpose of the *National Courier* was to bring the mind of Christ to bear on today's events. The biweekly, a nondenominational tabloid, used the talents of more than eighty-five Christian journalists to report national, religious and church news within the Christian perspective. Unfortunately the *National Courier* never attained a subscription and advertising status where it was not a financial drain and eventually the newspaper was discontinued, its news section merged into the *Logos Journal*. Many of the *National Courier* field reporters are now authoring books for Logos.

LIF sponsors the World Conference in Jerusalem on the Holy Spirit. The first one in 1974 and the second a year later together attracted more than 9,000 delegates to Jerusalem and Tel Aviv, Israel to praise the Lord and learn more about what He is doing in the world today. Additional conferences were sponsored in 1976, 1977 and 1978. A 1977 conference was also held in Lausanne, Switzerland.

"We arranged for these conferences because we felt God wanted us to," explained Dan. "However, we were totally unprepared for the enormous response and apparent impact they had both on the conferees and the nation of Israel. The Holy Spirit gave us wisdom and, as a result, a significant number of Israeli leaders came away from the event with a fresh understanding of Christianity."

Missions and seminars in foreign countries to promote worldwide unity and understanding in the Body of Christ are sponsored by LIF as a part of its international ministries. In addition, the fellowship supports ministries involved in interdenominational worldwide church renewal. Foreign translations of Christian books and the *Logos Journal* as well as frequent distributions of free literature, books, magazines and newspapers in foreign countries is another ministry of LIF.

"Probably one of the greatest contributions to the Christian world," predicts Dan Malachuk, "will be the Logos International Study Bible. A scholarly group of Spirit-filled men and women, representing the major historic churches, will cooperate in developing this most important Holy Spirit reference commentary. It will be the first international study Bible ever published with a special emphasis on the ministry of the Holy Spirit."

Dan believes this new study Bible will be another means of bridging the doctrinal differences among Christians, unifying them as one in the Holy Spirit.

A vital aspect of the LIF ministries is the thousands of prayer partners who voluntarily remember the worldwide ministry of LIF in prayer each day. Dan emphasizes that "Viola and I and the trustees realize that unless the Lord builds the house the labor is in vain. We understand we are capable of making mistakes, and these we have made. We also realize that we cannot ask friends to assist us in this ministry unless we have first committed our own lives and finances to it."

Currently, there are 140 employees in the Logos ministries. Most of the employees, according to Dan, are there because the Lord wills it so. Many report feeling definitely led to work at Logos.

"We know," asserts Dan, "that Logos is not a one-man ministry. It's a team effort, a practical expression of the Body of Christ at work."

Dan adds, "The cooperative efforts of friends and prayer partners, the hundreds who give monthly of their resources, and the Logos employees who gather daily for prayer and praise all join together to make Christ known to the entire world. Who is Logos International? As one of our authors said, 'Just a great number of King's kids.' "

The Lord has blessed. Some Logos books have sold over two million copies while others have hit the one million mark. A visiting evangelist remarked at a Logos prayer meeting, "The Lord shall do astonishing things." The comment has proved true. The Lord has worked amazing miracles in the short life of LIF.

"Write the vision, and make it plain upon tables that he may run that readeth it," the prophet Habakkuk said. And Dan praises the Lord, "For He has given Logos International Fellowship the vision of communicating the gospel of Jesus Christ throughout the entire world, and of bringing together the people of various nations and denominations so that they might become one in love and purpose. The Lord has done astonishing things and will do more to bring this vision to fulfillment."

And now Logos and the People of HOPE have been given a new vision, a new responsibility by the Lord—the bringing together of the Body of Jesus Christ through Jesus rallies similar to Jesus 78 at Giants' Stadium in the Meadowlands at East Rutherford, New Jersey. Plans were set in motion immediately following Jesus 78 by Dan and Jim Ferry for not only additional but bigger rallies in the name of Jesus Christ, the great Unifier, Savior and Healer—the King of kings and Lord of lords.

"And others," prophesied Dan, "will share the vision for stadium meetings around the world."

CHAPTER 5

People of HOPE

The Reverend James J. Ferry, a Roman Catholic priest, was a pioneer in the charismatic renewal among Catholics along the eastern seaboard of the United States when it took sheer courage even to acknowledge association with charismatics or Pentecostals. Father Jim, as he is affectionately called, is a man of courage and deep spiritual conviction when it comes to faith in Jesus Christ and the work of the Holy Spirit. So much faith did Father Jim have that he sought and obtained permission from the Newark archdiocese to leave parish work for prayer house pioneering.

Father Jim had reasons to believe God wanted him in the charismatic renewal movement. While assistant pastor at St. Anthony's church in Northvale, New Jersey, he had hundreds of Catholics attending charismatic prayer meetings. He began a House of Prayer core in Stanfordville, moved to Goshen, then Suffern, all in New York state, before finally locating in January, 1972 in Convent Station, New Jersey. There was no guaranteed

PROPHECY IN ACTION

income, only dependence upon the donations of those who came to the House of Prayer to seek the Lord. He had been invited to Convent Station by the Sisters of Charity who maintained headquarters there. Here he founded People of HOPE—People of House Of Prayer Experience.

The People of HOPE is a Catholic charismatic community of prayer and evangelization which has had for the past seven years a history of evangelistic outreaches, principally in northern New Jersey. Today there are 269 adult members who have made a commitment to the covenant community of People of HOPE. Jim Ferry is overall director of this community which is modeled after the Word of God community in Ann Arbor, Michigan.

The community's Newsletter for the Fall of 1977 states: "We look with gratitude to the Lord for all He has done since November 1, 1970 when the beginnings of HOPE took form in the little House of Prayer in Stanfordville, New York, through the times in Suffern, in Goshen, in Jersey City, and in all the outreaches of those seven years. . . . And we look with great gratitude to the Lord for what He is doing in us now in the new People of HOPE which took form when the first group made their public commitment on May 1, 1977."

Father Ferry stated in a recent interview that he sees the community of HOPE "like a new wineskin to contain the power of the Spirit." He added, "Everybody wants the renewal to go into the parishes and that's fine. But the renewal needs the double thrust provided by the existence of alternative modes like the covenant community."

Father Jim warns of a danger of parish-centered

44

renewal becoming "nothing more than a Thursday night Holy Spirit devotion." He says, "That would not perform the function God wants of it: renewal of the whole church."

Liz O'Connor, writing in *The Long Island Catholic* of April, 1978, quotes Father Jim as describing the covenant as "a group of people who've experienced renewal in their lives and who have decided to live their commitment to Jesus by committing themselves fully to each other. It's not a commitment to structure but to people." Because of this depth of commitment, the community admits married people when both spouses freely choose to join.

The small groups into which the community is divided are called households and they meet weekly for two hours. Such a meeting generally is comprised of group prayer, teaching and sharing in groups of men and women. The full intent and purpose of the household is to support one another in living the Christian life.

Father Ferry explains that "members of the community clearly make a significant commitment in terms of time with the emphasis on relationships. We commit ourselves to support one another. If we have needs, the first ones we go to are our brothers and sisters in the Body."

One of the ministries at the Renewal Center of the community is the Saturday seminar. These seminars open in the morning with prayer, then teaching followed by sharing in small appropriation groups, private prayer and then Mass at noon. Following lunch there is more prayer, teaching and sharing in small appropriation groups, a healing service and Scripture sharing.

The seminar often is broken down into separate teaching tracks with subjects such as Inner Healing, Yielding to Praise in Tongues, Call to Personal Holiness, A Day for Separated and Divorced Men and Women, and A Day for Single Men and Women.

People of HOPE ministries also include "Life in the Spirit" seminars which are held in six HOPE centers in conjunction with the weekly Thursday evening prayer meetings for a total of some 12,000 people. The six HOPE centers, all in New Jersey, are: St. Antoninus Parish House, Newark; Holy Trinity Hall, Westfield; Immaculate Conception Church, Norwood; Xavier Center, Convent Station; Sacred Heart School, New Brunswick; and Star of the Sea Church, Bayonne.

A Life in the Spirit Seminar is a seven-week course which is termed by its sponsors one of "the best means of coming into a life lived more deeply in the Holy Spirit." A flyer announcing the seminars asserts, "The seminar is an opportunity to find out more about this life and how to take the first steps in a new relationship with the Lord Jesus. The seminar helps one to experience a fuller release of the Holy Spirit in life and to live a deeper Christian life."

Then there is a Jesus Week given in local parishes under the direction of HOPE by a team from HOPE community working with the pastor and parish leaders. The chief focus of the week is to proclaim Jesus as Lord. It's a parish or area-wide mission, a tool for evangelizing, so that all might be renewed by the power of the Spirit of Jesus for the glory of the Father.

Usually the initial contact is made by the pastor of the

parish who, in seeking the spiritual renewal of his people, writes his request to the HOPE community, and the community responds by arranging a meeting with the pastor. The first meeting is to determine exactly what the pastoral leadership of the parish expects and the attitude toward the Catholic charismatic mission and regarding the HOPE team. It is explained that an offering is taken each night of the Jesus Week by the team to cover expenses of the week and to support HOPE. A stipend is not ordinarily required of the parish.

There are additional meetings to form a joint committee from HOPE and from the parish to make preparations for the week. During the month prior to Jesus Week, flyers are printed and distributed, news releases and letters of invitation sent out and newspaper ads for local and diocesan press are prepared.

The services during the week are more or less structured in that they follow a pattern of opening with music and prayer, a featured speaker, a witness or testimony and concluding prayers and hymns. People who wish to do so may pray to be baptized in the Spirit. Opportunity for the Sacrament of Penance is offered each night and Mass is celebrated on the final night. Topics of the featured speakers include "God's Love," "Accepting Jesus as Savior and Lord," "The Gift of the Spirit" and "Healing the Whole Man."

God has brought about miraculous healings in answer to prayers at the community's various outreaches. For instance, a letter from the Bob and Ginny Gallic family in one of the Newsletters states:

"Jimmy, our two-year-old son, was truly rescued from

death. After surviving three serious operations in a space of three weeks and being overcome with various infections and pneumonia, he was scheduled for a fourth operation to close a hole in his stomach. Through the prayers of many that operation wasn't necessary because the hole was healed by God without surgery. All the fears of Jimmy coming home, weakened mentally, spiritually and physically, were dispelled when he walked out of the hospital and went home to a peanut butter and jelly sandwich."

"The Healing Workshop given by Father Francis MacNutt in the summer of 1977," recalls Father Ferry, "prepared two members of our community to step out in a new faith for healing. In recent months the Lord has anointed other members of our community with gifts of healing."

At St. Antoninus Church in Newark, an inner-city parish, where Father Ferry is administrator, a healing service is held after the 11 A.M. Sunday Mass on alternate Sundays. Healings do happen. A man, for instance, was healed of cancer of the prostate during prayer for healing. Here, too, in the inner-city, parish members of the community of HOPE work. Other members of the community staff Sacred Heart School in New Brunswick. They also offer various renewal opportunities at their Renewal Center in Xavier Center on the campus of St. Elizabeth College in Convent Station. A 28-minute movie, *Go Tell Everyone*, on evangelization in the modern world is available. The film portrays the experiences of community members and others through their ministries and outreaches.

People of HOPE

One of the truly outstanding spiritual highlights was the community's participation in the Jesus 78 Rally at Giants' Stadium in the Meadowlands Sports Complex. In no small way, the rally was a dream come true for Father Ferry, who in June of 1977, at a national meeting in Ann Arbor, Michigan, was appointed to the National Service Committee of the Catholic Charismatic Renewal of the United States. Father Jim recalls how he used to drive by Giants' Stadium and tell himself what a wonderful tribute to the Lord it would be if charismatics could fill that stadium one day with a tremendous rally for the Lord. The thought even boggled his mind. But he is a man of faith.

He had been hosted by the State Conference of Catholic Charismatic Renewal in Brisbane, Australia and several other leadership conferences and priests' days of renewal in Sydney and Melbourne. He also had attended with members of the community the 1977 Conference on Charismatic Renewal in the Christian Churches in Kansas City, Missouri, giving talks and conducting workshops in addition to serving in the Word Gift Unit and other roles. Then there was the Regional Eastern Catholic Charismatic Conference in Atlantic City in 1977. There on the boardwalk he met Dan Malachuk. They had met at other conferences but this meeting between the two men would prove to be an historic one because their conversation that day on the boardwalk turned to holding a combined Catholic-Protestant charismatic rally.

Father Jim thought of Giants' Stadium as the site for a giant rally. He thought too of all such a project would entail and it seemed a gigantic task for two men to attempt. Then he recalled Psalm 37:4-5: "Take delight in the Lord, and he will grant you your heart's requests. Commit to the Lord your way; trust in him, and he will act" (NAB).

There on the boardwalk the two men vowed to push forward with plans for Jesus 78. Actually, the vision of Jesus 78 came from the openness of Father Jim to respond to the call of the Kansas City conference. In a sense, his vision was an extension, now coming alive in the covenant community of the People of HOPE, of a body with one mind and one heart.

The vision of unity of the churches was to have concrete expression in (1) a vision of the body with one mind and one heart to sponsor and service Jesus 78 and (2) a public celebration of unity in the belief that Jesus is Lord in Giants' Stadium on the eve of the anniversary of the foundation of the church of Jesus Christ. A longtime desire of Father Jim to sponsor a day of praise and worship in Giants' Stadium became a reality when the Spirit called for this day to be an interfaith celebration.

The strong community life and experience in refined teamwork in the ministry of the People of HOPE was the basis of many of the contributions of the community to Jesus 78. The experience gained by leaders of the People of HOPE in formation of community—Body—as they grew from a tiny group in a House of Prayer into the covenant community was brought to Jesus 78. In their ministry, the People of HOPE have always worked in teams, as a body. Practical experience had been gained through their work in giving parish missions "Jesus Week," special evangelistic outreaches in halls, band pavilions and so forth at the Jersey shore in summers, also from serving in various capacities in regional Catholic charismatic conferences and from ministry in their own retreat renewal center, city parish and in a parochial school.

Knowledge of certain basic elements needed for a group of individuals to become a body was part of the experience of the leaders in the People of HOPE. The necessity to make agreements with each other as sponsors and in teamwork and service were important elements. Other elements included realization of the importance of sharing and planning at meetings in preparation for the event, agreement to a definite order and leadership in meetings, agreement to come to decisions through discernment and to accept discernment as the leader of the group.

The organizational structure of both the Catholic church and charismatic prayer groups with Catholic leadership had a network effect which made communications to these groups easy and efficient. The fact that the People of HOPE was a part of this network aided in speedy promotion of Jesus 78 and in obtaining volunteers to serve on the day of the rally in Giants' Stadium. A "Jesus 78 Update Bulletin" was issued several times during the months of preparation for Jesus 78 to keep these people informed about developments. The Bulletin was especially effective in making groups in different areas aware of "One in the Spirit" nights throughout the whole area.

Many of the services of the day at Giants' Stadium were headed by members of the People of HOPE—services which required organization of a large number of people into a body with one mind and heart. The ushers were the largest group in this type of service. Others included music, operation of the scoreboards, security guards, first aid helpers, collection security, liaison with television and radio, press relations, arrangement for Spanish translations, distribution of the Kansas City film and many minor details associated with such a giant rally as Jesus 78.

Then there were other services effectively accomplished jointly with Logos International Fellowship. These included administration in planning, recording registrations for admittance to the rally and distributing tickets, promotion, program selection, hosting and coordination of "One in the Spirit" evenings.

The joint sponsorship developed into a beautifully coordinated effort, directed and strengthened through the power of prayer and the blessings of the Lord on a day set aside to praise Him and glorify His name.

CHAPTER 6

The Press Conference

It didn't take the word long to spread among the members of the press at Giants' Stadium that Ruth Carter Stapleton was holding a press conference at 9 A.M. Her press conference was scheduled ahead of the regularly scheduled noon conference because she was to be an early morning speaker and wished to be free after giving her message. Although the sister of President Jimmy Carter, Mrs. Stapleton has much going for her in her own right which makes her in great demand in Christian circles.

Ruth began her ministry teaching Bible classes. From there she moved out to speak in churches and interdenominational retreats and conferences in the surrounding area and then across the country. She has expanded her outreach across the world to laymen and leaders of foreign nations. As may be discerned from her books and writings in national publications, her ministry is inner healing which is concerned with the healing of emotional problems through prayer.

A native of Georgia, Ruth now lives in Argyle, Texas

with her husband, Dr. Robert Stapleton, a retired veterinarian. She is the founder of Behold, Inc., a lay evangelical and teaching mission headquartered at Holovita, a thirty-acre Christian counseling and teaching center in Argyle.

Members of the press were anxious to know what effect being the sister of the president of the United States had on Ruth's ministry. Actually, she said, very little, although occasionally she was told that she shouldn't go here or there because she was the sister of the president. But that did not influence her. She explained, "Christians must manifest their Christianity in everyday life. 'Go ye into all the world.' "

A member of the press noted that Ruth was the only woman speaker on the Jesus 78 program. He asked if that bothered her. "Oh, no, not at all," she answered. "I work better if I have a man or men working with me. I come alive then. I personally don't think I'm strong enough for overall leadership."

When asked her opinion on the grass-roots movement to bring Catholics and Protestants together, Mrs. Stapleton was enthusiastic in her reply. She explained that she had been working with Catholics and Protestants for many years. "The walls that once separated now are crumbling," she said.

A final question asked at her press conference was, "Would you explain inner healing?"

"Inner healing," she said, "is healing deep inner problems. Negative experiences in early life. Inner healing cuts through all barriers in negative minds and heals them. Perfect love would cast out all these inner feelings of negativeness and fear. Imagine Jesus' love. His love works on that reverse level."

Mrs. Stapleton was asked if she had spoken to Larry Flynt lately. She has consistently counseled him in his spiritual life. She told the press conference that she talked with either Larry or his wife almost every day and he is trying to learn now if and how Jesus can use him.

Another member of the press started to ask Ruth a question, but Father Jim Ferry called a halt to the conference, explaining that she was due to address the rally in a few minutes. The highlights from her address are reported in chapter 9.

The later noonday press conference, with the other speakers in attendance, seemed to focus on women in leadership roles in the charismatic movement, the effect of the rally on bringing the Body of Christ together and how much of a spiritual effect the rally would have on those attending. Father Jim Ferry, pastor of St. Antoninus Parish in Newark, New Jersey and director of the People of HOPE, answered the first question concerning the women's role in the charismatic renewal.

"I believe that women have a very special leadership role in a community that overemphasizes male leadership overall," he said. "Now that's just our community—the People of HOPE—and it's the leading that we are following. However, I see women having a very special role in the charismatic renewal. The People of HOPE Community was started mostly with religious women. I believe that women have a very special role in the church. I think that it is going to be unfolding.

"How will it develop? Our own special feeling is that we

look to the man. I think that in our churches in many ways the women have taken the lead and men have not, except for the clergy. I am talking about lay leaders. They have not emerged in the past. However, I am seeing it happen now. Male leaders are emerging and they are being supported very much by women. I thank God for women in our community who exercise leadership. And I thank God for Ruth Carter Stapleton who led us today."

One of the reporters wanted to know how many were in the stadium and how many would be there by the day's end. Another reporter asked what areas were represented.

Bob Armbruster, publicity director for Jesus 78, answered that, according to figures given by Meadowlands officials, 54,015 people had entered the stadium by noon. Dan Malachuk, president of Logos International Fellowship, Inc., of Plainfield, New Jersey, answered the second part of the question. He said that the inclement weather had held down the attendance. More than 60,000 registrations had been received and some of those ticket holders were not in attendance as yet. Moreover, a few thousand perhaps had intended to come and register at the gate as they entered the stadium, but the weather had kept them away.

In regard to the areas represented, Dan explained, "We understand there are bus groups from the Baltimore-Washington area, also from areas in Pennsylvania. Groups have come from Long Island, from Providence, Rhode Island, and from the Boston area. I would think our strongest pull came from within a 300-mile radius. And, of course, I can't forget Charlotte,

North Carolina and the PTL people."

Dan also answered the next question from a reporter who wanted information on the financial aspects of the rally: How much did it cost to put it on and would there be a deficit or profit?

"We originally began with the idea that the rally would draw about 30,000," Dan explained. "As it began to grow, so did the expenses. I believe that the last figure we have is that our expenses are running about $110,000. Now that covers the rental of the stadium, plus security, plus electricians, plus carpenters, plus stage, plus sound, plus everything else. And so, on that basis, with the many thousands of free tickets, plus the fact that many came in groups of ten which gave them a registration rate of only $2.50 per person instead of $3.50, the real net comes to about $1.80 per person.

"We will be happy to break even. But the idea was not that it would become profitable because Logos International Fellowship, like the People of HOPE, is a non-profit ministry. Any surplus, if there is any, will be used to provide free literature for other cities. We have a prison ministry. We have an overseas ministry for translations of Christian literature and other ministries. The People of HOPE are involved in Newark and the inner-city with their ministry and other outreaches. So there will be ministries to be funded from any excess of income over expenses.

"But we are really grateful that the Lord allowed us to have this rally. We don't know yet what's going to happen. If the stadium officials had told us the rally would cost $110,000 in the beginning, we might not have gone ahead with it, but we were kind of eased into it. I suppose it is just like everything else. When you start out you just begin and all of a sudden they start giving you the bills and then you learn where you really stand.

"We are grateful for all those who have come today. It's a rather historic meeting because it's probably the largest group of its type ever in an interfaith way. And so we are grateful that it could happen.

"We already are realizing some of the fruits in the form of requests from some other cities asking, 'Can it happen in our city?' We certainly will help those cities desirous of holding such a rally in every way we can."

A questioner wanted to know if either Dan or Father Ferry could assess the impact of the rally on the ecumenical movement at the grass-roots level, particularly in the immediate area. Father Ferry volunteered to answer.

"I think this was like a watershed," he began. "It was the gathering of people together. This day was planned and prepared for by over thirty-one meetings called 'One In The Spirit' nights. These were held in different areas. People came together to hear a Catholic priest and a Protestant minister, to hear testimonies and to see the movie on the Kansas City charismatic conference in July of 1977. Hundreds of people came from their local areas.

"Today is such an inspirational day. We are meeting next Tuesday, the steering committee that put this together, to ask, 'Lord, what do you want us to do from here?' I think the next thing we have to do is to bring the pastors together in a new way. By pastors I mean the people who have pastoral care for other people. As the pastors come together the congregations will follow. We are looking for God's wisdom on that."

The next question was directed to Jim Bakker, founder of the nationally-known Christian television talk show, the "PTL Club." The questioner wanted to know when Christian leaders would start talking about the love, grace and mercy through Christ Jesus, and His atonement for sin for one and all on the cross at Calvary. "When," asked the reporter, "are they going to start talking about the need?"

Jim Bakker paused a moment before the microphone and then began his answer. "I believe that is where the church is right now. I believe this is the message of love. In fact, that is what I will be preaching on in a few minutes. You see, Jesus Christ prayed that we would all be one and I believe that any prayer that Jesus Christ, the Son of God, prays will be answered. Today we are seeing that answer take place right out there in that stadium because we are coming together as one. This is the fulfillment of the prophecy of Joel and also the New Testament prophecy that in the last days God would pour out His Spirit upon all flesh."

Jim then referred to a question asked earlier about women in leadership, saying that the prophet Joel had prophesied that God would pour out His Spirit upon the handmaidens, upon your daughters and sons. "We are seeing that in our own ministry at the PTL Club," Jim said. "We are using more and more women in very high places. Just within the last two days we promoted two women to assistant vice presidents. We have seventy husband-and-wife teams working for us. That's another thing they say can't happen. It won't work. But we believe that this is the day of the Holy Spirit moving. By His will, not our will any more. And His will is that women be elevated. And we see it taking place in the world, but we are seeing God doing it. I think it is a far more substantial elevation when God elevates."

As Bakker moved away from the microphone, questions began from three separate parts of the room. Bob Armbruster, conducting the conference, promised that everyone would have his turn and selected the question from a gentleman who wanted to know if the renewal was something that would continue on after the rally.

Dan Malachuk prefaced his answer with the suggestion that the reporter put the question to some of the people in the stadium. "We have represented here various aspects of different ministries," said Dan. "Jim Bakker performs a very vital ministry as an evangelist, using television. He is like John the Baptist crying in the wilderness and bringing forth large success.

"The one thing we have discovered is that unless what happens here is related to a church body, it is not going to produce the fruit that God wants. Many have come here as strangers, unrelated to a New Testament society, or community or church. We see a problem for them unless they get rightly related with a Christian group. We are not only interested in people coming to know Christ or being filled with the Holy Spirit, we are interested, too, in them coming into a growing relationship with God."

Dan explained that he was an elder in his church and that he believed in church government. He also believes that all of us must be related to some authority and, as we are related to an authority that God has established, an authority under the Holy Spirit, then it moves forward and we really can accomplish the work of God. "So this is not the end," asserted Dan. "This is but a beginning of what God wants.

"I would say that in the coming days, months and years stadium meetings will become commonplace. I believe it was one of the bishops who mentioned, 'Isn't it wonderful that the Christians are back in the stadium? But not to be eaten by lions.' No! Rather for the coming together and giving a demonstration. I thank God for the bishop making that statement.

"We must be related to one another. What is crying in the hearts of lay people and clergy open to the things of God's Spirit is that unity begins in all of us at every level. I believe we have to see that. It is not enough that an ecumenical conference decides how we can get together. It is very important that we decide it's time to get together and do it, rather than just waiting and waiting and waiting."

Almost as if in substantiation of what Malachuk had stated in regard to people having an experience at the rally, but not having it last, George Gallup, Jr. found this very thing happening to unchurched individuals. Gallup found that more of the unchurched than the churched have had sudden religious experiences. They are all charged up, but with no place to go. Dr. Gallup noted that a key criticism of the unchurched in regard to religious institutions is that "Churches have lost the spiritual part of religion." About one of every five unchurched persons who indicated they had "problems with churches checked a statement which said, 'I wanted deeper spiritual meaning than I found in the church or synagogue.' "

Father Michael Scanlan, a Franciscan priest, president of the College of Steubenville in Ohio, and immediate past chairman of the National Service Committee of the Catholic Charismatic Renewal in the United States, elected to answer the longest question put to the panel at the press conference. The reporter prefaced the question with the statement: "The whole theme of ecumenism is that the Body of Christ is broken. It has been broken in the Christian community since the Reformation. The Catholics go back to their church from a meeting like this one and believe that they are the one true church and those outside the church are not part of the Body. The dialogue between Catholics and Protestants has been going on for 400 years. No matter what happens at the grass-roots level in terms of emotions, these questions separate theologically."

After that long preface came the question: "I just want to know if it is possible for a rally like this to make these questions easier and bring us one step closer to a solution."

Father Scanlan lost no time in pointing out what he believed to be an error in the questioner's preface to the question.

"First of all," he said, "I don't think your statement on church doctrine is correct from a Catholic point of view. The Vatican Council documents clearly that the one true church is not confined to the Catholic Church, that indeed all who are committed to the Lord Jesus Christ can belong to the one true church. The Vatican Council document said that the true church subsists in the Roman Catholic Church. Now that means that it has its roots in it. But in no way does it mean that it is confined to it. So, therefore when we preach the Body of Christ, we are preaching that we believe, and I believe as a Catholic, that all who belong to the Body of Christ have salvation.

"I think since the Vatican Council document it has been developed into a far more living principle. I think it is very important for us to distinguish between evangelism and proselytizing. The Christian churches have tended to proselytize, which means to get people into 'my denomination,' or into 'my particular group,' or 'parish.'"

Father Scanlan pointed out that evangelizing is basically bringing people to Jesus Christ and bringing them into the Body of Christ. He said that he believes true evangelism always has an ecumenical dimension to it. Never is it saying that those evangelized can only come with me. They are saying the fullness of life is in the Body of Jesus Christ.

Concluding his remarks, Father Scanlan said, "Now within the Body of Christ there are many ecclesiastical communities. There is much participation. I believe the message we are giving today is a message that gives people both an awareness of that fact and starts moving them to broaden their horizons; not to confine themselves to their particular denominational church but, indeed, to get their denominational church more into the fullness of the Body of Christ."

As Father Scanlan concluded his comments, Father Ferry indicated he had some thoughts he would like to express. He told the members of the press, "We had a good experience last night. We got together and prayed and the word God gave us was, 'Who moved the stone?' We are finding out that for centuries we have been building up a lot of stones, but right now the stone isn't there any more. Something is happening in the Body of Christ that witnesses to the removal of the stone. This is prophecy in action that we are seeing out there in the stadium. The people are the greatest prophecy because many have come here for some reason. That reason may be possibly that they are not going to other churches but are searching for one. I don't say that we are starting a church.

"What we are saying is that God is doing something in the world. This is a sovereign move of the Holy Spirit. Something new and special is happening and I don't know where we are going. I don't have a road plan. I know who we are going with—Jesus Christ. He's leading. We're going to the Father. The evidence of the Holy Spirit is all around. The only way we know is that Jesus gave us guidance. 'By their fruits ye shall know them.' I see fruits of love and peace and joy. It's a new day.

"Now the stone has been removed. But the Lord wants us to unbind one another. As Lazarus came forth, he came forth bound. The Lord didn't unbind Lazarus. Lazarus had to be unbound. We have to do that to one another. I think we have to say, 'Where are we going? Where are you leading, Lord?' This is historic, but it's only a stepping stone. It's an arch to the future. We are going to see a greater day."

As Father Scanlan left the microphone Bob Armbruster announced, "I would like to ask Father

Bertolucci what he sees as the significance of this event."
Father John P. Bertolucci is pastor of St. Joseph's
Roman Catholic Parish in Little Falls, New York. He is
a former vice-chancellor of the Albany diocese. He
presently is a member of the steering committee for the
Bishops' Liaisons to the Catholic Charismatic Renewal.

A big, bearded man, Father Bertolucci began his
comments by explaining that something happened to him
while coming in on the plane to the airport, something he
would report in his message that afternoon. "But I will tell
you first," he said. He then explained that the stewardess
was serving drinks aboard the plane and asked him if he
would have something.

"I didn't have my collar on," explained Father
Bertolucci. "I was a little bit more relaxed that way. I said
that I would like a glass of wine. She served me and then
asked if I was a man of the cloth. I was immediately
embarrassed and answered, 'Yes, I am.'

"She wanted to know what kind of cloth. I told her I was
Catholic and she said she was Presbyterian. I asked her if
she loved the Lord. 'I do,' she replied and I told her I loved
the Lord too. She went on with her duties then, but
returned later and sat down beside me. 'Would you pray
for me?' she asked, explaining that she was suffering from
a skin problem.

"Right there in the middle of the plane I laid hands on
her and prayed that she would be healed. For a moment
my Catholicism and her Presbyterianism weren't lost or
denied or anything like that. They were still there. I was a
Catholic priest and she was a Presbyterian stewardess."

Father Bertolucci went on to explain that what had

happened was that Jesus Christ, who was common to both of them, had brought them together on another level of relationship. They were responding to basic human needs and calling for the power of Jesus Christ to heal those needs—to meet those needs—and to bring them closer together in a love relationship.

"Today," said Father Bertolucci, "I am still a Catholic and I know that today she still is a Presbyterian. She might even be in the stadium because I gave her one of our folders. But something happened that brought us closer together, that has really brought both of us to a point of convergence in Jesus and that has reawakened in us an awareness that God heals today.

"Now that is significant. It breaks down a lot of walls, a lot of hostilities, a lot of barriers and it brings us closer to the oneness Jesus is praying for. The second thing I want to say is that this is God's work. You can't sit here and plot it. What is significant out there in the stadium is that we are tapping prayer power.

"Finally, I want to emphasize this. When you get Protestants and Catholics, Anglicans, Orthodox and nondenominationals praying together, watch out."

The next questioner wanted to know what kind of media coverage was being given the rally. Dan Malachuk volunteered to answer. He said that if he was correctly informed, "We have NBC, CBS, ABC, Metro television networks, radio stations, PTL, a television station from West Germany and a number of daily and weekly newspapers, along with some magazines."

Dan postulated that by the time the rally has been fully covered by the news media, from at least seventy to one hundred million people could possibly view it. It had been announced that CBS was doing a special one-half hour presentation which would be televised on the network the next week. It was possible that one telecast could reach anywhere from four to forty million people.

"I would say," proffered Dan, "that to reach that many people on a $110,000 budget is a good investment. But above the visibility," he added, "there is something when the Body of Christ comes together. On the day of Pentecost, why was it that not just ones and twos got saved, but thousands were saved because God is a God of demonstration. He wants a demonstration here, not only in this city but, I believe, in every city of the world.

"I don't think we have a right to be content with what happens here. Our hearts should be reaching out and our visions expanding to believe that God can bring people together, just as He has done here, in a demonstration in the Soviet Union, in Poland, in South Africa, in every nation of the world. I believe it can happen in every nation if and when we get together. It is up to us. God is ready. He is waiting for people He can trust."

As Dan finished, it was announced there was time for one more question. A reporter wanted to know how the Jews might take the success achieved in converting Jews to Christianity. Jim Bakker replied by saying that "We are interested in reaching all—Jew or Gentile—because we believe in what we are doing. We believe that Jesus Christ is the Messiah."

Jim explained that his findings in his own personal relationship with the Jewish people had convinced him that he is not out to convert Jews. He added that if they do get converted to Jesus Christ and find Jesus, the Messiah, along the way, then he is very happy. He told of a Jew, Gene Goldberg, who came to the PTL program to talk about the Holocaust. They spent many days together, sharing as they talked. After several weeks Gene said, "You know, I can't understand it, Jim. How come you haven't tried to convert me?"

"We were becoming very close friends," Jim told the press conference. "I believe the real job of the truly born-again Christian is to love every human being on earth and to reach out with that love because God is love. I love the Jew just the way he is and I know God loves him too. I love everyone just the way they are. I believe that is the state the church really needs to come to. Let the love of God shine through and leave the results in the hands of God."

CHAPTER 7

The Day at Jesus 78

The seven-hour charismatic Jesus 78 Rally found many of the people arriving at Giants' Stadium shortly after six A.M. They came by air, bus and motor car, bringing lunches in coolers, wicker baskets and paper bags. Many carried umbrellas. The deaf and other handicapped came, too, some with walking sticks and in wheelchairs.

The stadium filled rapidly amid an atmosphere of suppressed excitement, a joyful outlook and great expectation, despite leaden skies forboding a wet day. Events would prove it to be a day whereby the fruits of the Spirit—love, joy, peace, longsuffering, gentleness, goodness and faith—as recorded in Galatians 5:22, would be manifested.

Exactly at nine o'clock the audience was led in singing, "Rejoice in the Lord Always," with the words of the song flashed on the giant computerized scoreboards at each end of the stadium. Leading the singing were the Reverend Ray Baker, associate pastor of Tabernacle Church, Melbourne, Florida and Father Philip Merdinger, associate pastor of St. Antoninus Roman Catholic Church in Newark, New Jersey and the HOPE music ministry.

Used normally to give the scores and pertinent information of Giants' and Cosmos' games, the scoreboards now came alight with passages of Scripture and words of song and praise to life's greater winning score in the victorious Jesus. All eyes focused on such phrases as, "Jesus is Lord," "Hallelujah," "Praise God," "Rejoice," and "One in the Spirit." At times they pulsated with the name, "Jesus."

A member of the religious press remarked, "Seeing Jesus exalted in such a manner is like being a forerunner to the time, 'When every knee shall bow and every tongue confess that Jesus Christ is Lord.' " Another reporter commented, "Wouldn't the Christian athletes get a thrill seeing these scoreboards today?"

As each major speaker stepped to the podium, the scoreboards beamed a remarkably realistic photograph-like image of the individual.

Lifting the hearts and spirits of the assembled was the singing of such songs as "Worthy is the Lord," "Hymn of Glory," "This Is My Commandment" and "Come and Worship." During the initial period of praise and song the audience was captivated by a squirrel running about the field. The little fellow put on his act just before Father Michael Scanlan gave the opening message of the day.

Prior to Father Mike's message the assemblage, with uplifted hands, sang reverently, "Oh, How I Love Jesus," followed by the reading of Psalm 100. As Father Scanlan approached the podium, the people stood and sang, "Spirit of the Living God."

Speaking on the unity of the Spirit, Father Scanlan noted that in such unity there is not rivalry, no complaining and not a sense of being number one. He said we want to belong to the Body of Jesus Christ, content ourselves with putting that Body first. During his message, the Scripture John 17:21 was displayed on the scoreboards; also, "Create in me a clean heart, O Lord." Following his message, which is given in greater detail in chapter 8, there was a prophecy in which the audience was told, "I called you to be committed to one another, lay down your lives for one another." And displayed on the scoreboards were the words, "Mourn and weep for the Body of My Son is broken."

Mrs. Ruth Carter Stapleton, the second speaker of the morning, had really set the tone for the day at an early morning press conference when she said, "The true message of Christ—which is unconditional love—breaks down barriers between religious groups." In her message that morning she said that she believes "our calling is to go into the world to accept, to love . . . not to just share verbally." She was given a standing ovation at the conclusion of her talk which is discussed in chapter 9.

After more singing and praising, the executive director of the New York City Council of Churches, the Reverend Dan Potter, closed the morning session by leading the audience in prayer.

During the lunch period a press conference, reported in detail in chapter 6, proved interesting and informative. Also at the noon hour recess the lunch counters and book and record tables became beehives of activity. Despite the rush by the people to make their purchases and return to their seats, and despite the difficulties encountered by the volunteers in coping with such a crowd, there was no rowdiness, rudeness, pushing, shoving or impatience. A security guard, observing the orderliness and patience of the people moving about, commented, "I've never seen such kindness and politeness in so big a crowd. Everyone seems to be looking out for the other fellow's welfare instead of trying to get there first himself."

Beginning the afternoon session, Andrae Crouch, a soul gospel singer and winner of Grammy and Dove awards, was introduced and received a thunderous ovation. Interspersed with his songs, he told the audience, "I'm glad to be here. I'm grateful for the Lord Jesus Christ and for what He means to me. I'm grateful because when I was nine years old He saved me and I haven't regretted one day walking with the Lord."

He said that when he was eleven years old the Lord gave him the gift of music. "My dad needed a piano player in his church," Andrae recounted. "He laid his hands on me and prayed for the gift of music for me and two weeks later I started playing the piano and the Lord began to give me the feeling for music. You see, the Lord knows each of our needs. There are so many times we feel that God cannot do things but He can do everything.

"The wind is blowing. It's a little chilly to some people but you're on fire. I'd like to sing the song, 'If We Can't Move in Jesus We Cannot Move at All.' "

Andrae sang his songs, including "Amazing Grace," with the audience spontaneously joining in singing several with him. He closed by telling the people, "If you don't know what God can do, I'll tell you what He did for me. He healed my wounded spirit. He mended my broken heart."

Jim Bakker, founder and host of the PTL television talk show, gave the audience an account of a conversation he had with God. Many took that message home with them and wrote later to explain how it had affected their lives. The conversation, condensed, was "You love 'em, Jim, and I'll judge them." Bakker's theme was "Love Is Now." His message is treated in more detail in chapter 10.

Father John Bertolucci had the huge crowd roaring "Amen!" and thundering "Yes!" in answer to his questions. He said, "I pray that God will give the churches wisdom to end even the eucharistic disunity which we now experience." He called tears a gift of God, saying, "There's a time for crying about disunity in the church."

Near the end of his message, Father Bertolucci asked, "Who's going to win the world for Jesus?" Back came the thunderous reply, "We are!" Once when he had his listeners in deep prayer, then singing in unison, "Holy Spirit, Come," the sun broke through the clouds. Many saw the incident as a direct, visible answer to their prayer—the descent of the Holy Spirit. Some reported seeing a dove circling the area. A report on Father Bertolucci's message is in chapter 11.

Terence Cardinal Cooke of New York made an appearance near the end of the rally and spoke briefly. He said, "It is a great joy for me to be here on the eve of Pentecost and see this tremendous witness to the power of the Holy Spirit moving in our time." He added a loud, "Hallelujah!"

Archbishop Peter L. Gerety of Newark spoke briefly,

PROPHECY IN ACTION

addressing his remarks in Spanish to some 2,000 Hispanics attending the rally. As a salute to the Hispanics the audience sang, "Tu Eres Mi Dios—For You Are My God" and "Alabaré." The archbishop, speaking in English, described the rally as "one of the largest interfaith gatherings in the history of the world." He added, "Nobody could have gotten us together on this eve of Pentecost except the Spirit of God. . . . We are praying for visible unity among Christians just as the community at Jerusalem gathered to wait and pray for the first Pentecost."

Protestant leaders, commenting briefly, were Logos author Harold Hill, noted for his *King's Kids* books, Mike Evans, leader of the Messianic Jewish community B'Nai Yeshua, and Earl Prickett, vice president of the Full Gospel Business Men's Fellowship, International.

The power of the messages at the rally upon the lives of the individuals attending is best judged by the comments made at the rally. For instance, Wilma Supik, religion editor of the Bergen *Daily Record* (New Jersey), commented, "As I sat up in the third tier for most of it, I just didn't believe it. I didn't believe looking around and seeing all these people. Many, many times I've been in Yankee Stadium and I never thought that I would be in a major stadium filled with Christians loving the Lord and with such great faith. I didn't think it could happen."

An unidentified deaf woman was crying with joy because the messages were translated into Spanish and also in sign language for the deaf. She exclaimed, "Just think, they didn't forget a thing!"

Jana Childers of radio station WPOW was amazed that

74

it didn't rain. She said, "I see the highlight as bringing together so many different groups of Christians in praise and prayer to the Lord Jesus Christ."

Galatians 6:8 tells us that "If he sows in the field of the flesh, he will reap a harvest of corruption; but if his seed-ground is the spirit, he will reap everlasting life" (NAB).

Roving reporters from Logos and the People of HOPE mingled with the audience, obtaining their reactions and comments. Their interviews with a number, prior to the beginning of the program, revealed a variety of religious backgrounds, covering a wide geographical area.

Sister Rosalina, a high school teacher in a parish church in Philadelphia, said, "I think it's wonderful that Father Ferry and Dan Malachuk could get together on this. I think this is the seed for the unity of the Spirit, and I hope the seed grows into a sprout and the sprout into a vine."

Mr. and Mrs. James Mate came "to praise Jesus." They are schoolteachers and attend the Episcopal church in Helmetta, New Jersey.

Ronnie Wiggins, a young black man from Chicago, came to Jesus 78 with a group from New York Teen Challenge. He said, "I've been a Christian for one and a half years. I came to the stadium to get blessed. I'm open for whatever Jesus has for me."

Marjorie Banaut, a former Presbyterian missionary to the Sudan and licensed practical nurse, commented, "I came to be spiritually filled for my work in the hospital because I can't go to church since I work on Sundays." She came with a bus group which left Margaretsville, New York at four-thirty in the morning.

PROPHECY IN ACTION

Father John Pierce, OFM, from St. Ann's in Fairlawn, New Jersey, was baptized in the Spirit in August, 1973, an experience that had a great effect on his life. He said, "It opened the Scriptures to me, gave me confidence in myself, my preaching and my prayer life." He has been a priest since 1963. Interviewed prior to the Jesus 78 services, he said, "I believe many things will happen today. There will be inner healings and physical healings, praise, encouragement, guidance. You know, St. Francis was charismatic all the way."

As the day progressed, comments and interviews began to reflect people's impressions of the day and the program. Sergeant Major Anthony Bontempo of the Salvation Army, Irvington, New Jersey Corps, came with Lieutenant Donald Thompson who said, "This day is great. The Lord always does big and great things." The Salvationists brought a group of thirty of their people. Bontempo is a member of the Full Gospel Business Men's Fellowship, International and has been a Christian for three years. He commented, "It's a little cold today, but it's warm in my heart anytime I get together with other Christians."

A young, black youth leader, Gordon Leslie, from Antioch Baptist Church, Springfield, New Jersey brought three junior high boys with him who were with "Youth on the Move for Christian Ministries." He said, "It's really thrilling. I bet the devil is hot as heck; he doesn't like it at all."

Willie Rouse, a Baptist and a truck driver from Brooklyn, had a seat on the third tier in the stadium. His comment: "I love every bit of it. It's beautiful."

Bill Bell of East Brunswick, New Jersey is a plant manager. He was in on plans for two of the "One in the Spirit" nights. He said enthusiastically, "It's a great day. I was at the Atlantic City conference last fall. I thought then, 'Wouldn't it be great to have all Christians from all faiths together?'"

The Reverend Paul Ruter of Belleville Reformed Church said Jesus 78 gave Christians "high visibility. . . . It's like the Israelites camping on the plains of Moab. It really cheers me." The New Jerseyite added, "I appreciate these types of meetings very much but I am concerned about the equipping of the saints in the fivefold ministries—apostles, prophets, pastors, teachers and evangelists."

"I love the unity in the Spirit," said Claire Vutura of Smithtown, New York. She attends the Smithtown Gospel Tabernacle. Her friend from Sayville, New York, Elsie Marchelewski, said, "You look around you here and all you see is joy."

An oil burner mechanic, Jim Ravier is an elder in the New Jerusalem Evangelical Lutheran Church in Hellertown, Pennsylvania. His description of the rally was "Fantastic! The day is positively good; a good experience." A busload from his church came to the rally.

Dino Giambione from Brooklyn, an ex-con who was a collector for the Mob, accepted Jesus and now five or six of his gangland friends have found the Lord. Wearing a Jesus T-shirt, Giambione reported with exuberance, "This is great. It's fantastic! Jesus is wonderful."

Patsy Ciniello of Jersey City had attended charismatic conferences in Atlantic City twice and compared those experiences with Jesus 78. He said, "Atlantic City was big. But this is it! This really shows glory to God." With considerable emotion he exclaimed, "I've never felt better in my life. My son is here today and he is back with Jesus. Hallelujah!"

Sister Leonie, S.C.C., from Rockaway, New Jersey explained that she began with the Community of HOPE six years ago. Her prayer group, called "Christ the Light," began with fifteen members and the attendance now is eighty or more. Since receiving the Holy Spirit baptism, she found "The Scriptures have come to mean so much more to me. I never realized how important the Holy Spirit is." She added, "I enjoyed Ruth Carter Stapleton's message and I pray that the love of which she spoke will spread out like spokes from this stadium."

For more than ten years Haralynn Wighard had not been in a church or religious meeting. She saw a flyer for Jesus 78 and decided to come completely on her own. A thirty-year-old Ridgefield Park, New Jersey resident, she said, "The Lord spoke to me today. I feel wonderful. During a time of praise when I put my arms up in the air, I was healed of painful bursitis in both of my arms. God has such a wonderful sense of humor. He showed His reality by letting the sun come out during a time of worship."

Revealing comments were made by some people hurriedly leaving the stadium. Their names were not obtained. A man reported, "The Holy Spirit touched everyone. I'm looking forward to it happening in many cities."

A woman said, "I was overwhelmed. I've swayed back and forth from the Lord for years. I'm never swaying again."

A comment from a young girl: "Thrilling! I've been here to many ball games but being here for Jesus was much more thrilling."

From a guard on the field: "All the love that was here this day in the crowds was overwhelming."

The week following the rally members of the People of HOPE shared their reactions. Steve Buczek, who sat in the upper tier, explained, "It was quite awesome. The Pinkerton guards and the Meadowlands people couldn't believe all the order. I spoke to some of the guards. They were hesitant at first to commit themselves. Then they started to soften and relax. I could see in their countenances how the Lord was affecting and touching them. By the end of the day I think they were really touched by the Lord's love."

Dick Floyd: "I thought this is really what God has in mind for the world. Last Saturday in just looking at the people, I could get a complete vision of what God has in mind for His people."

Betty McElhill, one of the People of HOPE deeply involved in the planning for Jesus 78, commented, "What came to me during the day was how gentle the Lord is. Awesome is the way to describe the day for me. It was the most powerful day I've ever experienced in my whole life."

Students from the Holy Family Academy for Girls, Bayonne, New Jersey were ushers at the stadium. Sister Grace Eileen, S.S.J., reported, "Our girls were truly impressed and privileged to be ushers for such an historic day in the life of the Church."

Representative of the comments among the girls are

the following. A freshman found Jesus 78 "A very memorable day. It was a learning experience not only for me but for everyone who attended. It was really beautiful to see all the love, kindness and happiness that was in the Meadowlands. I couldn't believe it. I'm very interested in attending next year and bringing my whole family with me."

A sophomore was "very proud and very happy to be a part of Jesus 78. This experience was new and interesting to me. I was glad that I had time to do my own soul searching and I discovered new feelings within myself. I enjoyed the day very much and would like to do it again."

"To me, being a part of Jesus 78 was a privilege, a rare and unique one," commented a junior. She added, "I cannot express in words alone the joy and happiness I felt. The closeness of God I received not only through the speakers but through the friendliness the people had towards me was unbelievable. I'd like to thank Sister Grace Eileen for making it possible for me to go. I'll never forget it."

One reflection on the day which seemed to perfectly wrap up the whole purpose of Jesus 78 came from Mrs. Marcia E. Leahy, religion editor of the *Asbury Park Press*, Asbury Park, New Jersey. She wrote, "Those who deny the miraculous don't know much about journalism. As religion editor for a daily newspaper, I was responsible for objective coverage of Jesus 78. As a Christian, I was responsible to God for the job He had given me to do.

"I braced myself for what I knew would be an exhausting day as I logged countless miles between press box and field, juggling my dual role as reporter and photographer. I also knew the envy I'd feel toward those who came simply to enjoy. They were there to get blessed; I was there to get a story.

"But by the end of the day I realized that I'd enjoyed a sweet communion with my Lord like I had on no other assignment. That's the beauty of the Holy Spirit. He ministers where there is need, whether you are silently bowing before Him in the grandstand or tracking down the president's sister for an interview. That is the miracle of a loving, caring God.

"Down on the field at midday I noticed another photographer, obviously from the secular media. Her tired face reflected a life style radically different from the Christian walk. Her cynical expression reminded me of so many other journalists I've met on similar assignments. But as I watched her I began to understand that she was what Jesus 78 was all about. Yes, we were there for unity, but unity for its own sake is pointless.

"We were really there for her and for every other unbeliever in this country whose broken life can be transformed to the glory of God. We, both individually and corporately, must be an example of what can happen to a life totally submitted to the Lord. Such an example cannot be fragmented, and the unity of spirit displayed at Jesus 78 is evidence enough that God is beginning to piece back together the broken Body of Christ."

Through the comments of the interviewed and by pieces of conversations overheard it became apparent that everyone at Giants' Stadium for Jesus 78 enjoyed a rewarding day with thousands finding a new experience with Jesus. As the day drew to a close, Father Ferry who acted so ably as master of ceremonies, asked the people to clean up any trash they might have and place it in the proper waste receptacles. Stadium officials said afterward the stadium had never been left in a more orderly and rubbish-free condition.

The overwhelming consensus was, "Let's do it again next year."

PHOTO SECTION

Photos in this section taken by Logos photographers:
David Tommasino, Doug Klein, Tim Mirenda and Lin Bachert

Scoreboards in action welcoming the incoming people to Jesus 78 and crowd settling in their seats for 7-hour Rally.

85

Scoreboards at both ends of Giants' Stadium flash morning greeting to thousands attracted to Jesus 78 Rally, May 13, 1978.

Overall picture of people attracted to Jesus 78 in Giants' Stadium.

87

Group praying and praising at early morning prayer meeting.

Raising hands in prayer and praise in moment of spiritual exaltation.

(Reading Left to Right) Dan Malachuk, Father John Bertolucci, Mrs. Ruth Carter Stapleton, Father Michael Scanlan and Father Jim Ferry.

Dr. Kenneth L. Folkes, founder and pastor of Mt. Carmel Baptist Church, Bronx, New York, giving invocation.

Father Michael Scanlan delivering his message on **God's Priorities.**

A busy day at the book and record tables.

Mrs. Ruth Carter Stapleton defining her **Roots of Five Basic Truths.**

At noonday press conference, from left to right, Jim Bakker, Dan Malachuk, Father Michael Scanlan, Bob Armbruster (standing) and Andrae Crouch, gospel singer.

Andrae Crouch entertaining audience with gospel songs and testimony.

Jim Bakker expounding on his message **Love Is Now.**

PTL Club television cameramen shooting scenes to be used later on the PTL Club telecast over its network.

Father John Bertolucci emphasizing a point in his message on **Seven C's to Success.**

Scoreboard flashing theme of Jesus 78 Rally.

Buses lined up in Giants' Stadium parking lot after discharging passengers at the Rally.

Flyers used to publicize Jesus 78 Rally.

The Most Reverend Peter L. Gerety, archbishop of Newark, New Jersey and Father Ferry enjoy a humorous incident.

LOGOS INTERNATIONAL
JESUS 78
PEOPLE OF HOPE

Father Jim Ferry acting as Master of Ceremonies.

Terence Cardinal Cooke, archbishop of New York: "When you say 'Praise the Lord,'
you've said everything."

Mary Ann Jahr of *New Covenant* magazine: "Ruth Stapleton touched people personally."

Jana Childers of radio station WPOW, New York City: "I'm amazed it doesn't rain. Today's highlight is bringing all these people together to praise and pray."

Trenton Diocese Liaison with Charismatic Renewal, Father Jim O'Brien: "I'm especially impressed with the word of unity coming from the speakers and the prophetic warnings that the Lord wants to heal the divisiveness and make us one in Him."

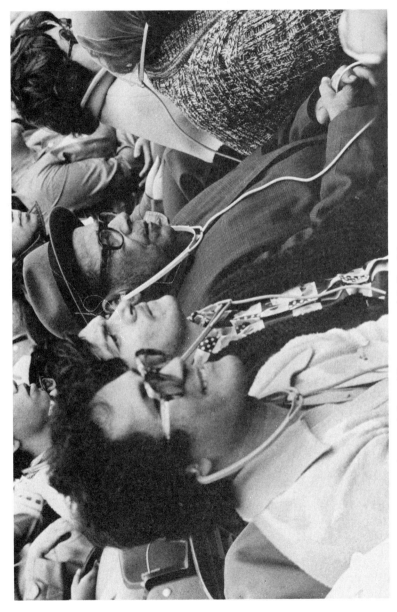

Some 2,000 persons listened to translations of the messages into Spanish.

Physical feeding as well as spiritual at the noonday recess.

106

A moment for solitary prayer.

An outburst of praise as the sun breaks through clouds.

109

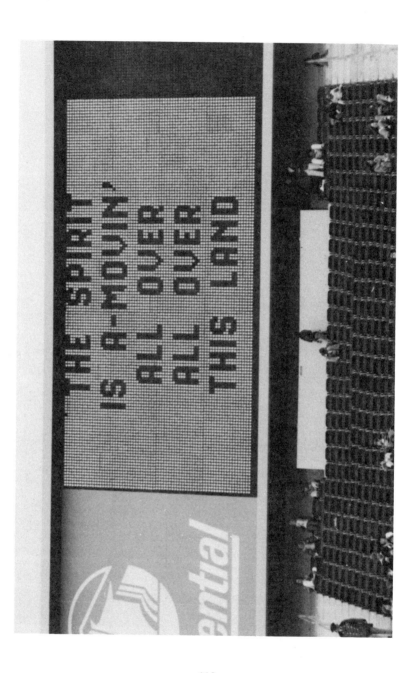

112

"Come, O Holy Spirit, Come."

"Suffer little children, and forbid them not, to come unto me: for of such is the kingdom of heaven" (Matthew 19:14).

CHAPTER 8

God's Priorities

Father Michael Scanlan in his message in Giants' Stadium stressed the priorities of God. He told the audience: "We are at the beginning of a giant movement of God, a giant undertaking by the people of God. We should experience some giant changes in our lives. We should be looking today to hear God's Word for us. We should be expecting to leave here different than we came. We've come because we believe that Jesus is the Lord, the only Lord, the Lord of the universe, the Lord of the whole world, the Lord of the Church. We believe that He is the Messiah, that He's anointed, that He's the Son of God, that He has been established as Lord of all and that He's living now among us. That's why we have gathered in His name."

Continuing, Father Scanlan said, "Secondly, we have come here because we have a desire to be united with all our Christian brothers and sisters. We want to be one."

He pointed out that our desire to be one may have come through God's Word, recognized in the living, anointed, inspired Scriptures in which God calls His people to be one. "That desire," explained Scanlan, "may have come through God's Spirit in our hearts, released within us, washing through us, baptizing us. It could stir in us that desire to be one. Or that desire might have come through seeing other people of God having the same commitments and same life as we have. Even though they were different, we recognized in them exactly what we were experiencing ourselves. And we said, 'We are one. We really are one.' Let's get on with it!

"We are here on this particular day," Scanlan said, "because tomorrow is Pentecost; because tomorrow we celebrate the Pentecost of the Church. And we are here because tomorrow we celebrate the day God poured out His Spirit, and now continues to pour Him out on all peoples, on all flesh, who come to Him. He wants them all together and all to respond to His Spirit. We know the prophecy in Joel is true. 'It shall come to pass in the last days, says God, that I will pour out a portion of my spirit on all mankind' " (Acts 2:17 NAB).

Scanlan explained that we believe that what man can't do, God can. We believe that man can't stop wars, solve all the problems of poverty, can't break down rivalry, feuds and mend together what's been divided, what has built-in passion, unforgiveness and resentment. But God can! God can lead us to be one people and overcome those kinds of problems.

He said unity is based on the Spirit of God. Ephesians 4 is life. We know that to be the reality of our lives. We are called to preserve that unity which has the Spirit as its origin and peace as its binding force. We seek unity, not based on negotiations, not based on theological discussions, not based on man's organization and not based on friendship though these can be good and helpful. We seek unity based on God's Spirit. What does the Spirit of God urge us to do? What does the Spirit of God say to us? The Spirit of God expresses the heart of God. The Spirit of God expresses the priorities of God. The Spirit brings to us what is first in God's heart, and that is what God is calling us to do today. To put first in our hearts what's first in His heart; to put first in our priorities what's first in His priorities.

What's first in God's heart? What is He calling us to this day? At this time, in 1978, God is speaking through the Scriptures, through the movement of His people, through the words of prophecy and through the movements of the anointing in our hearts. He's speaking one very clear word. That word proclaims that the most important thing in creation, and the most important thing in our lives, is to be the Body of Jesus Christ. All else is second to that.

The Body of Jesus Christ created by God the Father. All things are from God. From the Father came the Son, and the Son, Jesus Christ, was sent, as the anointed of the Father. 'This is my beloved son in whom I am well pleased.' He was sent forth from the Father to bring good news to the world; to show love of God to all mankind. Because of that He was beaten and crucified. He suffered to show the love of the Father for us, a love which would bring forth from Jesus Christ the Body of Christ. From Jesus Christ would come forth peoples of all nations, all colors, sizes and backgrounds who could find unity and meaning in His life. They would find the power to live, to rejoice, and find happiness. They would find the power to bring good news, solve the evil and problems of the world by living in the Body of Jesus Christ.

Scanlan explained that the Body of Jesus Christ, the unity of all who would be His disciples, of all who would be called—that's the treasure of the Father. That's in the center of His heart. That's what He most cherishes, and is the meaning of our existence. The answer to the world's problems, the answer to wars, persecutions, poverty and hunger, the answer to all the problems that surround us is only found in the Body of Jesus Christ. That is God's solution.

The prayer of Jesus in John 17:20-21 represents what's first in the heart of the Lord. "I do not pray for them alone. I pray also for those who will believe in me through their word, that all may be one . . . in that the world may believe that you sent me" (NAB). The absolute miracle of men being one, sharing one spirit, one set of ideals, and coming forth in one name—the name of Jesus. This miracle of the unity of Christian people was to show, before all else, that indeed the Father had sent Jesus Christ to us.

That oneness is in God's heart this day. And how is it to come about? We read in John 17:22, "I have given them the glory you gave me that they may be one." Not because they work it out for themselves, but because the glory of the Father comes upon them. The Spirit of God comes upon us, and we're anointed and empowered to be one.

Father Scanlan said, "Brothers and sisters, from all denominations, who are gathered here today and those who will see and hear this on radio, TV and movies, we have to see the facts. The facts are that the Body of Jesus Christ is divided. The Body is not one. In fact, over 250 different sects and denominations of Christendom are right here in the United States. When we reach out to the peoples of the world, in missionary endeavors, there are from 250 to 450 different interpretations and groups saying we're the ones you should go to.

"We have, in fact, a separated Body. First in the heart of God and what God treasures most is the unity, the vitality, the continuation of the life of His Son in the Body of Jesus Christ. But what is seen is not one Body. The same statements may be mouthed but we are not one Body and it's time we get on with that as the first task of all Christians."

Father Scanlan emphasized that God calls us to think every day, every moment and every prayer session, "Lord, what can I do to be a channel of your peace, a channel of your unity so that your Body may be one?" The Lord God calls us to see this unity. He calls us to draw ourselves so completely into this task of continuing the unity and building the oneness and vitality of the Body of Jesus Christ that it indeed becomes our frame of reference for life.

How can we do it? How can we move on such a giant task? For a moment dwell on a passage of Scripture, Philippians 2. Here we find how Paul instructs the Christians of Philippi to be one Body and urges them with deep passion for unity of the Body. We need to make those sentiments and passion of Paul our own. "In the name of the encouragement you owe me in Christ, in the name of the solace that love can give, or fellowship in spirit, compassion and pity, I beg you," says Paul. He didn't say I ask you, I guide you or instruct you, but "I *beg* you to make my joy complete by your unanimity."

What kind of unanimity? A unanimity of organization? Paul doesn't talk about organization. A unanimity of doctrine? That's important, but Paul doesn't talk about doctrine. A unanimity of friendship? No! Paul says, "by your unanimity, of possessing the one love, united in spirit and ideals."

"Possessing the one love, united in spirit and ideals." What kind of love is that? That's God's love. That's the kind of love God has for all Christians. That's the kind of love that seeks to build, draw forth, nurture and give ourselves to our brothers and sisters. It's not a love that has accusation. Satan's the accuser of the brethren. We learn that in the book of Revelation. Satan accuses the brethren. That's not our task. Our task is to build up the brethren, to love the brethren and to give ourselves to one another in a unity of spirit based on the same source. The same power will pull us together—the Spirit of Jesus, and the unity of ideals, gospel ideals.

The passage goes on: "Never act out of rivalry or conceit; rather, let all parties think humbly of others as superior to themselves." That's a big statement. What does that mean for us? No rivalry, no comparison! Not saying my group is better than your group. My church has more members than your church. My church is holier than your church. Let the football teams of the world be number one. We want to belong to Jesus Christ and not strive to be number one over other brothers and sisters.

"Put away conceit," Paul says. Put away self-satisfaction, and the sentiment that we have it all together, and we don't need one another. Put away the fact that we've got all the truth, all the life, all the church

and we don't need others. Put away the conceit that we've
set ourselves above others. Jesus told the Pharisees that
in having Moses and the prophets they didn't have the
fullness of life. He said that the very stones would cry out
to acknowledge Him as Messiah.

We should content ourselves in only one thing, that of
putting the kingdom of God and the Body of Jesus Christ
first in our hearts to comply with what's first in God's
heart. "Think humbly of others as superior to
yourselves," Paul says. Take the position of a servant.
Take the position of one who is serving his betters, of
wanting to build up and serve the needs of our brothers
and sisters worshiping in different churches, in different
meetings and whose worship we don't fully understand.
We are called to honor our brothers and sisters, upbuild
and speak well of them. We are not to let anyone make fun
of people in other Christian denominations. We are to do
everything we can to defend their honor, and their
commitment. We are to delight in the success of others.
We are to desire that the world know Jesus through our
brothers and sisters who may not be worshiping in the
same assembly as we are.

Does this sound like too great an undertaking for you
today? Well, Paul was ready for that response from the
Christians of Philippi. He writes that your attitude must
be that of Christ. In other words, what kind of standard do
you use? You should do this in the same way Jesus did it.
You don't have to do more than Jesus. You don't have to
lower yourself any further than Jesus. You don't have to
serve your brothers any more than Jesus did. You don't
have to wash their feet more. You don't have to give

yourself more than Jesus did.

Jesus, though He was in the form of God, did not deem setting himself above and outside of humanity because He was God. He didn't say, "No, I'm God, I won't associate with men. I won't take on the lot and task of men." No, while being equal to God, He put himself down and, as Paul says, "rather he emptied himself and took the form of a slave, being born in the likeness of men."

This is what brings back unity. When we put ourselves in service to one another. When we seek to rejoice in others' triumphs, mourn their failures, support their good projects and give our lives to what they're giving their lives to. That asks a lot, but that's the price of unity. It's what Paul teaches us in Philippians 2. How are we going to do that? I believe that God wants us at the beginning of this day to decide for His heart. I believe that God wants us to repent of the ways in which we may have divided the Body of Christ, the ways in which we have blocked unity.

I believe that God is saying to us this day that if we will decide to put first in our hearts what is first in His, if we will decide to repent, if we will decide to be servants of our brothers and sisters, that He will be able to release within us His Spirit of unity. He will be able to release in us the healing power of His love, and the power to change our hearts.

It is a matter of the heart before all else. It's a matter of our hearts being right before our Lord. I now have to ask you, after proclaiming this message, whether you're ready for that. Are you willing to decide to have God's heart, God's priorities, and to live to build up the Body of Jesus Christ? Are you willing to decide to repent, to repent of every way in which you may have hurt Christ's Body and the ways in which you are preventing unity? Are you ready to let the Spirit of God move through you to heal your heart, to give you a new understanding of the unity you have with brothers and sisters in this stadium today? Paul says in 1 Corinthians 12, "You are the body of Christ."

We are the Body of Christ today. Look at that. Look at all those untold thousands, over 60,000 here already who are putting up their hands, wanting to be the Body of Christ—wanting to make that kind of decision.

All right, let's pray together. Speak from your hearts to the Lord.

"I'm sorry, O Lord, for hurting Your Body. I'm sorry for any of the times that I've engaged in ridicule of other Christians. That I've engaged in slander. That I've been in cold indifference ignoring them and ignoring the work of God in their lives. I'm sorry for the jokes that I've been a part of that weren't funny, for the rivalry that I've engaged in. For conceit. For not caring enough about my brothers and sisters. For not caring enough about Your Body. For not seeking Your heart and putting first in my heart what's first in Your heart.

Lord God, forgive us. Forgive us that we haven't cared enough. Forgive us that we haven't mourned enough and wept enough over the broken condition of Your Body. That we've been too caught up in our own concerns and our own organizations and projects and churches. Lord God we want to be called forth into the center of Your life. We want to be called forth into Your vision of what is important. Lord God forgive us and release in us Your healing power, Your power of love this day. Break into our hardened hearts. Break into our hearts of wood and stone and give us a heart of flesh.

"O God, You said that whatever we ask in Your name would be given to us. That whatever we agree to, according to Your Word, according to what You want for us will be given, and we believe this day, Lord, that You're going to give us that unity. That You're going to move us on the way to a oneness in the Body that we've never known before. Lord God we want to come on fire this day." Father Scanlan asked the people to open their hearts to the healing power of God. He asked them to touch their brother and sister on either side of them.

"Just touch them," he said, "so that you're praying as a body. You're praying as people who want to be part of the Body of Christ and not simply individuals. I would ask that this whole stadium start praying in the Spirit of God. Start calling the Spirit of God to flow into the center of your hearts." He then continued his prayer, "Create in us a new heart, O Lord. Create in me a new heart, O God. Lord God, let Your Spirit flow because Your followers have decided for You this day. They've decided to put first things first. They've decided to put first things first. They've decided to be the Body of Christ. They've decided to give their lives to that. Lord God, let Your Spirit of unity flow through them. Let Your Spirit of unity, Your Spirit of fire flow through them. Lord God, we believe that this is a new Pentecost. We believe in what You do in our lives.

"Praise You Lord Jesus and thank You Lord Jesus for being our head and Lord. Thank You Lord God and bless Your Holy Name."

CHAPTER 9

The Roots of
Five Basic Truths

Ruth Carter Stapleton, in her message, enumerated five basic truths concerning Christ's dominion over all the emotional conflicts and facets of life. She began her talk with a prayer which expressed an expectancy of healing from Christ through the Holy Spirit.

"Heavenly Father," she prayed, "we thank You that by the Holy Spirit You will be touching each one of us in some special way. Heal our bodies, heal our minds, our emotions and break down any barriers that may separate us from You, that we will be more open to Your love. We claim this healing for each one of us, in this hour, in the name of Jesus. Amen."

In explaining how she came to a realization of the five basic truths, she related several personal experiences. On one occasion she was seated next to a young man in an airplane. It was a long trip so, after chatting with him for quite some time, she asked about his belief concerning God. He shared some of his experiences, philosophies and ideas. She asked if she might diagnose him. He answered,

"Yes."

"Well, you are a Christian but not a very good one," Ruth said. "You don't really have too many roots. Your basic belief is in Jesus. But if you are going to have joy, have a good relationship in your marriage, know how to relate to your children and experience God's love, you've got to have some roots."

He wanted to know how he could obtain these roots. She shared some of her experiences with him. "As a result," says Ruth, "we now see each other frequently. His spiritual roots are getting so deep that I'm beginning to ask him questions."

That conversation caused her to reflect on her own life. She recalled that her theology had been very limited. Therefore she was constantly reacting to *people*. If they didn't believe as she did, she thought something was wrong with them, consequently she became very upset inside.

Then one day she discovered that the reason everyone upset her about their beliefs was because she herself didn't know exactly what she believed. Her roots weren't deep even though she had traveled, gone to every meeting she could find, listened to many different people and read numerous books. Finally, she became so confused with a conglomeration of everybody's theologies that she decided to empty herself of everything and go directly to the Word of God. She said, "Lord, teach me by Your Word. By the Spirit of Christ that is within me, teach me what is truth."

She explained, "That was really the beginning of roots for me because everything I began to incorporate into my spiritual life was something given to me from God's Word by the Holy Spirit. As I went to the Scriptures I found five basic beliefs that I could cling to and know as truth for myself.

"The *first truth*, a truth that consoles me at times when the world tries to sway me back and forth, is the truth that Jesus Christ is the Son of God. There is no doubt in my mind about this. As I relate to Jesus, the spiritual Jesus, I also know that He is the Son of Man; and I relate to the physical Jesus who walked on the earth. That brings me into His incarnation."

Continuing her explanation, Ruth said, "The *second truth* I've found is one that enables me to have a lot of practicality in my life. It's the truth that Jesus Christ has won dominion over heaven and earth. In Him is the victory because He is Lord. That's more than just a spiritual truth. That says to me that Jesus has won dominion over illness—physical illness. And Jesus has won dominion over emotional illness. He's won dominion over depression, over the need for sleeping pills and tranquilizers. He has won dominion over conflict and hostility."

Ruth said that when this truth began to take hold of her, she realized that in Jesus she too had dominion as she stayed in Him. This opened a whole new realm for her life. Why? She confesses, "I was one who had depression. I was one who took sleeping pills. I was one who had to have tranquilizers. I was one who sought peace and joy in ways outside Jesus. Now my life moved into a relationship in which I said, 'Jesus, touch those hurting areas in my life. I know it's not my inheritance in You that I should hurt, that I should have conflict within.' "

It was then that she began to take Jesus, through a sanctified use of her imagination, into every area of her life. In her imagination she moved back into those areas where people had hurt her. There she saw Jesus, holding that hurting little child inside her and she was able to say to each person who she imagined came before her, "In Jesus I forgive you." In this way she began to learn that *forgiveness* is one of the greatest experiences one can have in life.

It was around this time in her life that Ruth had what she describes as "a kind of strange experience" with a man she chanced to meet on the road. She was driving to a meeting when a tire blew out. It caused the car to zigzag crazily and come close to turning over, finally ending up in a ditch. A man in a car behind her stopped to see if he could be of help. He offered to take her to the next town. Just then a pickup truck that had been behind the man's car pulled up and stopped. Two teenagers alighted from the cab. One said, "Lady, we can fix your tire."

"This gentleman has offered to drive me to the next town," Ruth said. "I'll get someone from the filling station to come and repair the tire."

"But, lady, we'd be happy to fix it."

Ruth was in a hurry to get to the meeting. She turned to the man and said, "You take me into town for my meeting while they fix the tire."

The gentleman took her aside and warned, "But, lady, they will steal your car. Or they'll take your tires."

"I don't think they will," Ruth replied. "Besides, I don't really have the time to spend with the tire. My meeting is so important."

The man turned to the boys and said, "If she's going to leave you in charge, let me pay you for doing this for her."

"Oh, no, sir," one of the boys said. "We want to do this just because we want to do it."

At that the man and Ruth Stapleton left. He wanted to know how long her meeting would be and she told him about an hour. "I'll wait for you," he said, "because I know your car is going to be gone when I drive you back." Ruth remonstrated but when she came out of the meeting he was waiting for her.

Later when they began driving back to the car, the man warned, "Now don't be surprised if your car is gone. I hope you have insurance. I hope your husband is a gentle, kind man."

"You know," Ruth told her audience, "he was really disappointed when we came over an incline in the road and saw my car sitting there. I got into the car and everything was fine."

The man insisted on following Ruth back to a service station, explaining, "You'll need to get a spare tire for your trip home."

They stopped at a filling station where Ruth suddenly realized she had neither money nor a credit card. She asked the attendant if he would accept her personal check. "I don't have any identification," she said. The attendant said he would accept her check. The man entered into the conversation then, insisting that the attendant charge the tire to his credit card, taking the card from his wallet.

"I told the lady I would accept her check," the attendant said. "I don't need your credit card."

"But you don't know this lady," insisted the man. "She's a stranger. I don't know her either. What if the check bounces?"

The attendant said, "Listen, man, I told you I was going to take her check. If it bounces, that's my problem. I am going to do it."

Ruth saw the man again about six months later. He sought her out and shared with her an unusual story which she needed at that particular time in her life, she said, to have her own emotions healed. He told her that on the day her tire blew out, he had left his wife and children. He got into his car, carrying several hundred dollars in his wallet, and was going to drive until he reached some place where he knew his family would never find him. Then he was going to commit suicide.

The man had been in deep depression for many months. "I was driving down the road," he explained, "trying to decide which state I should end up in to take my life. Then I came upon you with your blowout. I became very confused because you trusted those guys on the side of the road, and then that filling station attendant trusted you. It was making me so upset because I used to be a church treasurer and I had embezzled $10,000 from the church. My biggest problem was that I never got caught. I had to live with myself. It got so into my system as guilt that I got paranoid. I felt that everybody was looking at me, seeing that I was a thief. I got to the place where I couldn't trust anybody because I couldn't trust myself."

The man told Ruth that after leaving her he made up his mind to return to the state where he had embezzled the money and confess to them at the church. He went to the minister and confessed the theft. The minister told him, "I don't have any authority but I'm going to take this before the board. I know they'll honor this confession and they'll forgive you."

The minister did take it before the board and they said, "You came on your own. We forgive you."

The man then went home and told his wife she should leave him, confessing the theft of the money to her. "Oh, my goodness," she said. "Is that your problem? I thought you didn't love me any more. I'll help you. We'll work together and we'll pay the $10,000 back."

He told his wife he had one more person to go to. He had to see his boss. "I know he'll fire me," he said, "but I have to tell him because my job is bonded." He went to his boss who, after hearing his story said, "I'll take the bonding myself, personally, because I can't allow the company to bond you any more and I don't want you to quit your job. This is honesty like I have never seen before."

Ruth Stapleton explained to her audience that this man's experience helped her to really believe that the principles that Jesus teaches truly help us to win dominion over every conflict in our lives.

She found a *third truth* as she continued to search the Scriptures. This truth released her from "that feeling of a man without a country, or a woman without a country." There is a verse in the Psalms, she explained, which says, "I knew you before you were ever conceived in your mother's womb." In reading this, Ruth says, "I knew for the first time in my life that I was not an accident. I knew that I belonged and it was the beginning of my learning to relate to other people.

"I could look at others knowing that no person is an accident. There's a plan and purpose for each life. And I found that plan and purpose to be for one important reason—that we may be transformed into the image of Jesus. That's the reason we walk this life; so that everything within us can be broken down, that we may be an expression of love to our fellowmen.

"The Scripture says, 'Love the Lord, thy God, with all thy heart and love thy neighbor as thyself.' Knowing that Jesus loves me gives me that desire to love everybody else and to love my neighbor as myself. This is a truth that I am still working on."

Ruth came to a *fourth truth*—"In all things give thanks to Christ." She began to incorporate this truth into her everyday living, saying, "I thank God for this trouble. I thank God for this problem. Because I know that in *thanking God* for it, good can come of it."

About the time she was building her roots on this truth a tragedy occurred in her household. Her oldest son, then fifteen years old, was run over by an automobile. He suffered a concussion and was sinking into a deeper and deeper coma. Before she learned of the accident, her husband had been called and taken to the hospital. The person who came for her said, "Mrs. Stapleton, you've got to get to the hospital as fast as you can."

Before she could leave for the hospital she had to get a baby sitter for her other three children. She drove for the baby sitter screaming at the top of her voice, "Oh, God, why did you do this? Oh, God, how could you let this happen to *me*?" Then she thought of the Scripture, "In all things give thanks." She thought to herself, "Oh, Lord, no! I can't say I thank you for the accident."

She begged and screamed and pleaded. Finally she became so desperate that she said, "All right, God, I thank you for the accident for whatever good can come out of it. I thank you for every person involved in the accident. And I thank you for the one who was the driver of the car for the good that can come out of it for him."

Ruth admitted that it seemed a very foolish thing to say but after saying it she stopped screaming. All of a sudden there was peace in her heart and suddenly she heard herself singing, "I Have a Joy, Joy, Joy, Joy Down in My Heart."

She told herself, "Ruth, you're losing your mind. You know, you've freaked out. You're in shock. That's what's happened." Then she realized that though it was a peace that passeth understanding, there was a grace that had come over her. She realized that if her son, Scotty, lived, she'd thank God for the rest of her life. But if he didn't live, that he was totally in the hands of God.

She arrived at the hospital and found everyone crying, including her husband and her minister. She told them, "It's all right. It's all right." They thought she was in shock.

She spent all that night and the next day lying on a hospital bed next to her son's. "Really," she told her audience, "it was the most peaceful time in my life." The following day as she was lying there she heard a voice say, "Who are you?" She answered, "I'm your mother." Then came the question, "Who am I?" She told him that he was Scotty. He wanted to know what he was doing there. She explained that he had been in an accident. "Oh!" he

exclaimed. Then, "Will you get me some funny books?"
"He had a total recovery after a few hours," said Ruth.
"I think it was a miracle of God."
Ruth learned from this experience that we're not
thankful that we're sick. We're not thankful that there are
accidents. We are thankful that no matter how bad a
situation is, when we thank God we put Him into it. Then
His Spirit can begin to work. The healing can begin
because He is there. We are thankful for that and give
praise. We're not giving the power and the credit to
anything or anyone other than God through the Holy
Spirit.

The *fifth truth* was a truth which the apostle Paul
writes about in Romans. Ruth believes that Paul didn't
write this particular letter very early in his work because
"like Paul, in my maturity I have found something
wonderful. I have found that nothing, nothing in heaven,
nothing on earth, nothing in the past and nothing in the
future can ever, as long as I live, separate me from the
love of Jesus Christ."

Ruth believes that as we begin to truly experience this
love of Jesus, we take on a dimension that is the *call* for
this era. It's that dimension by which we become that
expression of Jesus Christ. As we look at the life of Jesus
we see one pattern after another. He walked on the earth,
up and down the hills, and on the mountain tops. And He
loved. He didn't just say, "I love you." He became that
expression of God, that *expression of love.*

He walked on forbidden ground in Samaria. He talked
to the adulteress at the well. There was no judgment.
There was no condemnation. He went down into the

taverns with the winebibbers and He loved them because He knew their broken hearts. He knew that *His acceptance* of them, *not* in *approving what they did* but in *accepting* them as *persons* was the thing that would bring them into *wholeness.*

"I think those who begin to have a spiritual reputation," said Ruth, "are supposed to go into the highways and byways and love the unlovely. I think this is one of the most important reasons why we have to have roots. We have to know the Word of God. When we move into these areas we have to have the strength of the Word grounded within us. And we need to have the wisdom of the Holy Spirit."

Ruth told of an instance where a minister warned her not to speak at a church in San Francisco. He said there would be drunks lying in the aisles, drug addicts sleeping in the pews, insane people from a nearby institution and all sorts of misfits. "Worse, the minister doesn't even proclaim the name of Jesus," said the minister. He added, "Besides, the press will be there to take your picture amidst all that and it will hurt your reputation."

She went to the church despite the minister's warning and found the situation as he had painted it. When the minister spoke, he didn't proclaim the name of Jesus. He was a *humanist.* But what he said to the people was, "We've got to love one another. You need me and I need you. When you come to my office next week don't come and say, 'Preacher, I need your help.' You come to me and say, 'Preacher, I need your help and I'm ready to turn around the other way.' "

Ruth said, "I listened to this minister talk to people who

had needs like I had never seen before. I said to myself, 'Thank God that I am here because if Christ is in me this may be the first time that Jesus ever got into this church.' I made a short speech after the minister called on me to do so and had the opportunity to tell those people how much I knew Jesus loved them. I told them, 'I know God is watching today and I know He is thrilled that you have agreed to come next Sunday and bring enough food to this church to feed 6,000 people on the streets. You may not be proclaiming the name of Jesus but, at least, you are feeding the hungry and loving the sick.' "

When Ruth was leaving the minister asked her, "Mrs. Stapleton, since they didn't throw you out, would you come back and hold an inner healing workshop in the name of Jesus Christ?"

Ruth told her audience at Giants' Stadium, "I believe with all my heart that Jesus was the expression of love and, if I am a Christian, I have to be an instrument of breaking down barriers." To explain her statement she told of an experience in Denton, Texas, near Argyle, where she has a lay evangelical and teaching center. She had gone into a shop to have a picture framed and noticed strange looking objects which reminded her of religious idols. She asked the young man waiting on her, "What religion are you?" He replied that he was a Buddhist and added that there was a colony of Buddhists in Denton.

"Well, I'm a Christian," Ruth said. "I'm opening up a Christian center here called Holavita. Why don't you bring your group one night and let's sing songs together?"

"Oh," he replied, "that would be fantastic."

When Ruth returned a few days later for her picture

the young man explained, "Mrs. Stapleton, my group of about twenty is very excited about meeting with you. But I think it's my duty to warn you that you better not have us. You are just getting started and people in Denton would be awfully upset if they knew we were going to your place. We'd ruin your reputation."

Ruth looked at the young man and thought to herself, "Oh, how much Jesus loves him! How good it would be to share the truth with him. We've got to be grounded enough in the Word that we know in whom we believe and that Christ's love is going to break down the barriers."

Ruth confesses that she keeps seeing how the Holy Spirit moves not only her but many into situations where He's calling each one to do his or her part in helping to break down barriers between races, denominations and cults in the furtherance of Christ's kingdom. Ruth explains "born again" as being born into the experience of Jesus Christ, identifying with Jesus and knowing what love is. Love that doesn't judge but breaks down barriers.

She explains, "We Christians have felt that it's our calling to be religious—to pray and praise, read the Bible, go to meetings and be at church every time the door is open. We are supposed to go to church, pray and praise and read the Bible. But that's not our only calling. Our calling is to go into the world, to love and, not only verbally, to share. They know when we love them. They know when we condemn them. By they I mean anyone who believes differently than we believe. My prayer is that we open our hearts to really and truly receive the love of Jesus Christ. The love that makes us secure enough to begin to express Jesus."

PROPHECY IN ACTION

Ruth closed her message with a prayer, exhorting the audience to pray, yielding their hearts to Jesus. She reminded her audience that the Scriptures tell us that "God will take that heart of stone and make it a heart of flesh." She expressed the belief that "in this moment every single one of us can have our hearts melted, that we truly can be open to receive His love."

She asked her listeners to remember that it's His love that is the healing power. She said, "If any of you are hurting in any way, if any of you are out of balance, if any of you are in conflict, now is the time for you to experience that love of God through Jesus Christ which heals and makes whole and redeems."

Her prayer was a moving communication with God.

"Heavenly Father, we ask You to open the heavens now. We ask, as we sit here in this stadium, that our hearts be opened, as the heavens are opened, and that Your love may begin to flow from one to another. In this stadium we call on that power of the Holy Spirit to touch the hurting hearts right now—hearts that are filled with hostility, hearts that have been broken and hearts that have never known love.

"O Jesus, we ask that You break down those barriers of hurt that we may be able to receive Your love right now. You may want to reach over and touch that person next to you. O Father, as You begin to melt that heart of stone, we ask that the spirit of love pour in. O Jesus, may we know Your love like we've never known it before. And as we experience Your love, will each one individually begin to think of those who have hurt us and silently say to them, 'I forgive you.' Maybe you can recall those who have been significant in your life, your mother, father; 'Mother, father, I forgive you. I forgive you for any hurt you have ever caused me.' Maybe there were brothers and sisters. Just say to them, 'I forgive you.' Whatever significant people you have known in your life, just say, 'I forgive.'

"O Father, as the Holy Spirit works within us right now, as we begin to experience this forgiveness, we ask the Lord Jesus Christ, we ask You to forgive us for every person we have ever hurt and we accept Your forgiveness toward us. We thank You that as *we forgive others, we* too *are forgiven.* And now, as we experience the freedom within our hearts, we ask, O Father, that You begin to draw us unto You, that we may know You. We pray that for everyone here. For each of you who never have said, 'O Jesus, come into my heart.' Maybe now your heart has been melted and forgiveness has taken place. Just say, 'O Jesus, come into my heart.' And say, 'O Jesus, I accept You as my Lord and Savior right now. I accept You as my healer and, O Lord Jesus Christ, let the Holy Spirit move within my body right now.'

"For anyone who has a feeling of illness in any way, pain in any way, any kind of infirmity, Lord Jesus, may every cell be quickened by Your power right now. May new life and new energy flow into every cell. We thank You that this process is beginning to work within our bodies now.

"Begin to give thanks and praise. Even if you don't feel anything is happening, give thanks to God and praise.

"O Lord Jesus, we've taken You into our hearts, into our emotions, into our spirits and into our bodies. We thank You now that You will integrate us into a wholeness of body, mind and spirit. We claim that wholeness. And, Lord, we thank You for the purpose of this integration; for Your healing within our lives that we may begin to be Your expression to a broken world.

"O Heavenly Father, as we move out from this day, rebuilt, renewed and made whole, we ask You to take us into the highways and byways, to help us face those who are in need and reach out a helping hand. O Father, we ask that You give us a condition within our hearts that we can commit our lives to feed the hungry, to give water to the thirsty, to clothe the naked and to heal the sick in the name of Jesus.

"O God, we claim that the barriers between religions and races are being broken down, so that Your Spirit of love can flow. We thank You, God, and we commit ourselves to this cause. But, O Jesus, let there be peace in the world and let it begin now. So now we offer ourselves as living sacrifices unto You to be made whole. In the name of Jesus bring us into wholeness for Your glory. Amen!"

CHAPTER 10

Love Is Now

In his talk, Jim Bakker dwelt on "Love Is Now." He mentioned that he had planned to give a message on "God's Timing" but on his way from the Carolinas to New Jersey, God impressed a different message on his mind. God laid on his heart that His message to the church today is that we love one another—that the charismatic love the noncharismatic. That the black love the white and the white love the black. That we reach out to love those of different denominations.

"When I arrived at Giants' Stadium," Jim said, "I realized, unbeknown to me, God had given me the very theme of the Jesus 78 Rally." He emphasized the subject, "Love Is Now," by explaining that "It wouldn't do me a bit of good to tell my wife I'm going to love her next year. *Love is now.*"

Before his opening prayer, Jim asked the audience to join him in reading John 17:21-23: "That they all may be one; as thou, Father, art in me, and I in thee, that they also may be one in us: that the world may believe that thou hast sent me. And the glory which thou gavest me, I have given them; that they may be one, even as we are one: I in them, and thou in me, that they may be made perfect in one; and that the world may know that thou has sent me, and hast loved them, as thou hast loved me."

Jim's opening prayer was brief. "Heavenly Father, I pray now that You anoint every ear that hears and every person within the sound of my voice. God, grant me a miracle. Don't let one person in this great stadium miss heaven. But, God, may everyone here be members of the Body of Jesus Christ. God, let the world see the love of God demonstrated. Not just talked about, but acted upon in the name of Jesus Christ of Nazareth, I pray. And all the people said, 'Amen!' "

Jim told his audience that, as a young man, he had the privilege of sitting at the feet of a wonderful pastor and his wife. They taught him about the love of God. The pastor's wife made Jesus so real to Jim that tears would stream down his face. He said, "O God, my prayer is that someday I may make the love of God real to people." Even then he believed that the world was hungry for that kind of love.

The pastor's wife talked about the Master of Galilee. One day she called Jesus God's beachcomber. She explained how beachcombers picked up bits of wrecked ships and pieces of wood. No one else saw any beauty in them but a beachcomber who, after picking up the bits of wrecked pieces, would make things of beauty out of them. She said that Jesus was God's beachcomber. He walked the earth, picking up wrecked lives and mending them. He loved the unlovely. He loved those no one else cared about.

"I want you to know now," said Jim, "that Jesus is walking all over this land. He is saying with outstretched arms, 'Come unto me, all ye that labor and are heavy laden' (Matt. 11:28). My belief in this hour is that the job of the Church of Jesus Christ is to *love now*, to *reach out now* to a sick and dying world. As it says in 2 Corinthians 6:2: 'Behold, now is the accepted time; behold, now is the day of salvation.' "

Jim told his audience that it was exciting to minister to his Catholic brothers and sisters. He reminded them that Jesus is coming soon and pointed to the rally as a sign of the soon return of Jesus Christ. He quoted Hebrews 10:25: "Not forsaking the assembling of ourselves together. . . but exhorting *one another*: and so much the more, as ye see the day approaching." He noted that strength will be in the unity of the Body of Christ.

"I wonder," Jim said, "how many times we as Christians have forgotten one another. The Body of Christ needs to care more. We need to care now. The Word says in 1 Corinthians 12:25-26: 'That there should be no schism in the body; but *that* the members should have the same care one for another. And whether one member suffer, all the members suffer with it; or one member be honored, all the members rejoice with it.'

"The Bible tells us in John 13:34-35: 'A new commandment I give unto you, That ye love one another; as I have loved you, that ye also love one another. By this shall all men know that ye are my disciples, if ye have love one to another.' Yes! Love is now. That's God's Word. Your Christian love will change others. It will transform lives."

Jim emphasized that one of the greatest deterrents to fellowship within the Body of Christ is the way people judge one another. He explained that people have come to him with criticism of someone he may have interviewed on his PTL Club telecast. They would tell him that the person was not right with God, or that the person had done this or that thing which was not Christian. It worried him so much that he developed ulcers. Then one day while he was waiting at a stoplight God made a deal with him.

God said very plainly, "Jim, you love them. I will judge them." He accepted the message as an admonition, followed it, and his ulcers vanished. He said, "I don't have ulcers any more. I sleep now because I can love everybody and let God judge them. Hallelujah!"

It says in Luke 6:37, "Judge not, and ye shall not be judged." After quoting this, Jim emphasized that if those who profess to be Christians would stop judging one another and begin to love, they could turn the world upside down.

"Many people," he said, "have felt that spirituality is pious praying, pious demonstration and pious worship. Jesus had much to say about pious demonstration without love. For instance, in 1 John 4:20 we read: 'If a man say, I love God, and hateth his brother, he is a liar: for he that loveth not his brother whom he hath seen, how can he love God whom he hath not seen?'

"God's Word tells us that if we love God, we must demonstrate that love. We are to love the Catholic priest, the Protestant pastor and those in other denominations.

If we can't love them then how can we love God whom we have not seen?"

Jim graphically pointed out that serving God is more than lip service. As an illustration, he said, "If I should say to Dan Malachuk over and over again, 'I love you. Praise God! I love you,' and if a member of his family or Dan should become ill, or they were in need, and I never did anything to demonstrate my love, I would show by my actions that I did not really love him.

"It's the same with God. If you love God, then love his family. The Bible says in Matthew 25:40: "And the King shall answer and say unto them, Verily I say unto you, Inasmuch as ye have done it unto one of the least of these my brethren, ye have done it unto me.' "

To expand further on Christians caring for others, Jim told of a missionary in India who spent years helping to feed little children. One day the missionary was driving down the street when he saw a man standing in the rain, waiting for a bus or cab. He stopped, took the man into his car, and drove him to his destination. Quite some time later when the missionary was trying to build a hospital in Calcutta, he was having difficulty obtaining a building permit. He walked into the office of the man who would issue the permit and seated behind the desk was the man to whom he had given a ride. The missionary obtained the building permit without further trouble. God honors your reaching out to others, Jim concluded.

The Bible tells us there's a time for this and a time for that and *now* is the time of *salvation*. There's an international salvation test. It's God's scriptural test found in 1 John 4:7-9: "Beloved, let us love one another: for love is of God; and every one that loveth is born of God, and knoweth God. He that loveth not knoweth not God; for God is love. In this was manifested the love of God toward us, because that God sent his only begotten Son into the world, that we might live through him." As a Christian, you will love. When love dies churches split, Christians disagree, homes are divided and people are hurt.

To know that we've passed from death into life is how we know that we are saved. How? Because we love the brethren. The Bible says in 1 John 3:14: "We know that we have passed from death unto life, because we love the brethren. He that loveth not his brother abideth in death." That is God's Word.

Commenting upon the fruit of a born-again Christian, Jim quoted from Galatians 5:22-26 which reads: "But the fruit of the Spirit is love, joy, peace, longsuffering, gentleness, goodness, faith, Meekness, temperance: against such there is no law. And they that are Christ's have crucified the flesh with the affections and lusts. If we live in the Spirit, let us also walk in the Spirit. Let us not be desirous of vain glory, provoking one another, envying one another."

"Such is the spirit of the born-again Christian," explained Jim. Then he asked, "What is the spirit of those who will not inherit eternal life? The lost!" He read from Galatians 5:19-21 in the Living Bible: "But when you follow your own wrong inclinations your lives will produce these evil results: impure thoughts, eagerness for lustful pleasure, idolatry, spiritism (that is, encouraging the activity of demons), hatred and fighting, jealousy and anger, constant effort to get the best for yourself, complaints and criticisms, the feeling that everyone else is wrong except those in your own little group—and there will be wrong doctrine, envy, murder, drunkenness, wild parties, and all that sort of thing. Let me tell you again as I have before, that anyone living that sort of life will not inherit the kingdom of God."

"I trust," Jim told the audience, "that if your life is not filled with the fruit of the Spirit this day that you will see the fruits of the flesh and death. That you will ask God to let you draw close to Him and become a part of the family of God."

He saw one of the problems today as the world inside the organized church. He said that it is so important that we, who claim the name of Jesus Christ, are not guilty of dividing the Body of Christ. He told of reading a newspaper in Charlottesville, Virginia which reported, "Prayer Guides Campaign of Born-Again Candidate." Jim said he had known the gentleman for years and considered him a wonderful man. The article quoted him as saying that "God had called him to run for political office." The only negative statement concerning his campaign was made by one of the largest religious bodies in America which opposed him, warning the people to beware of anyone who professed to be born again and entered politics.

"We see this happening," explained Jim. "Many times laws are passed in the church which were instigated because someone wanted to get back at another religious body. You cannot control what any religious body does or what someone else does, but we can control what we do."

PROPHECY IN ACTION

He referred again to loving the unlovely, pointing out that if we could love those who are into drugs and other sinful things we preach against, we could win them to Jesus and thereby clean up pornography, sin and lust at the root source—in their hearts. He called attention to the many Christians, perhaps some in the stadium, who had cried alone because there was no one to help them in time of need. Or when possibly they had fallen into sin or had something happen in their lives that people misunderstood, and others turned their backs on them. He cautioned the audience not to be guilty of doing the same thing. He said, "I know what it is to cry alone, to be misunderstood and written about in the press. Maybe your priest or pastor needs a friend, too."

He spoke again about the importance of showing the love of God to others—to those with whom we disagree or whose situation we do not fully understand. As an example, he told about an unfortunate incident in his brother's life.

"My brother was only forty years old when he died," Jim said. "I remember the last time that he ever went to church. For some reason my brother had rebelled against God. But that night my father and mother had brought him back to church. The offering was to be taken. My father was the head usher. Whether he was right or wrong, he felt it would be a good thing, since no one else was near, to have my brother take up the offering with him. He handed my brother the offering plate.

"Someone came up quickly, took the offering plate from my brother's hands and said, 'You're not fit to receive the offering.' My brother never walked into another church

148

the rest of his life."

A few years ago, as his brother lay dying of a rare disease, Jim went to see him in a Veterans' Hospital. "It was the first time in my life," said Jim, "that I was able to tell my brother I loved him. We had been separated so long by so much. I had prayed for him all his life. At every church service, I would raise my hand for prayer and say, 'Pray for my brother, Bob.' "

Just before his death, Bob Bakker dragged his weakened body aboard a plane and went to see a cousin who had shown him love and kindness. She prayed with him and he accepted Jesus Christ as his personal Savior.

After relating his brother's story, Jim reminded the people to "let's love and leave the judging to God." He recalled that God said, "If you don't aid those around you, if you don't love, you're not loving me."

Jim asked the people to close their eyes in a moment of prayer, examine their hearts and say to God, "If I am not loving You the way I should, help me now. Help me to begin loving my fellowmen. Help me to let Jesus Christ come through me to them." Then Jim urged everyone in the stadium to make Jesus Lord of their lives—"that before this stadium meeting is over," he said, "you will stand and say, 'Jesus is Lord of my life.' "

He closed his message with the following prayer: "Heavenly Father, we pray that You will examine our lives and that through this message, God has spoken to our hearts. O God, I pray that You will help us to realize that now is the day of salvation; that love is now and must be demonstrated. God, we pray that there will not be repeated cases of Bob Bakker who died alone because he did not feel the love of the Body of Christ. In this hour we will not figure out who is right and who is wrong, but we will love each other. We will be one in the Spirit that the world will see Jesus and fall at His feet. Amen!"

Jim asked the audience to say with him, "Love is now." He asked them to repeat it and then stand and say it one more time. Then, "Tell Jesus you love Him now."

Finally, Jim asked the people to throw their arms around a person sitting near, one whom they may know the least, and say, "I love you now. Praise you Jesus Christ. Glory hallelujah! Praise You, Lord God!"

CHAPTER 11

Seven C's to Success

In enumerating his *Seven C's to Success*, Father John Bertolucci explained that Christians must come together to discover their roots in Christ Jesus. He said that we cannot wash away our differences but must rise above them and learn how to communicate even within those differences. He stressed the necessity of emphasizing the primary truth of Christianity—*Jesus is Lord*.

He asked the audience if they didn't think a Jesus 78 Rally should be held in every stadium in the United States of America. There was a huge "yes" chorus. He added, "I hope I can come back here next year and each of you will bring one more person. I just thank the Lord that He has built so many beautiful stadiums around the world so that the people of light can gather and give witness to our belief in Christ Jesus."

He said that when he was in the charismatic conference in Atlantic City the previous October that something happened. He felt it was a sign from God that people

151

really better pay attention to what God is saying. "That prophetic word that is printed in your program," Father Bertolucci said, "is something that you should take home and study very carefully. It's a word that speaks of the need for all of us who profess belief in Jesus Christ as Lord to get on our knees and repent of the scandal of division. It's a word that even speaks about mourning, yes, even mourning for the division that is here. When I first heard that word in Kansas City—a prophecy given by Ralph Martin—I couldn't quite grasp its meaning."

Father Bertolucci went on to explain what happened at Atlantic City to impress upon him the full meaning of the prophecy. He was serving on a panel with David du Plessis and others, including Tom Twitchell from Rhode Island. The members of the panel were sharing on what the Lord was doing in their lives when Twitchell, pastor of a charismatic Presbyterian church, suddenly began relating his struggles in Providence, where his church is near St. Patrick's Catholic parish, a Catholic charismatic parish.

Tom told how he sent his children to the Catholic parochial school. His little son came to that precious moment in the class when everyone was preparing for their first Holy Communion. "But because of the terms of our discipline, discipline which at this point in time I do respect and submit to," said Father Bertolucci, "that little Presbyterian boy could not make his Communion with those other Catholic students. All of a sudden Tom Twitchell could feel the pain of division."

Continuing, Father Bertolucci said, "It is precisely at the table of the Lord that we feel the pain. And I believe we're supposed to feel the pain. I don't believe we're supposed to whitewash that pain at all. I long for the day when right here in this stadium, right here in the middle of this field, there will be a huge altar where all of us will be able to share in the body and blood of Christ Jesus. I long for that day. I hunger for that day. I thirst for that day and know that the Lord Jesus Christ wants us to eventually come to grips with the reality of the breaking of the bread. We're not there yet. We've only just begun.

"But at that point in time Tom Twitchell's little boy could not partake of Holy Communion in that Catholic church and neither were the Catholic boys able to partake of Holy Communion in that little boy's Presbyterian church. But you know it says in Ephesians 4:3: 'Make every effort to preserve the unity which has the Spirit as its origin and peace as its binding force.' "

Bertolucci proposed that the Spirit of God that day was going to give all in the stadium creative ways of demonstrating the unity that already existed, so that all might capture the unity that would yet be. He expressed a belief that God would give all creative wisdom from on high to create that unity, and preserve the discipline and obedience "to our elders which also is a part of the process."

He asked the audience if they agreed that Christians are to be obedient to their elders and the unity they are proceeding toward is going to come about on their knees, not in some kind of wishy-washy indifferentism. He said there still are differences between us and we must face that head-on. He explained that Tom and the authorities in the Catholic church began to try to find ways that somehow or another they could express the unity that already existed.

"After all," said Bertolucci, "look at what's going on in Providence, Rhode Island in that charismatic parish of Presbyterians and that charismatic parish of Catholics. They love one another. They work together and they have found a common relationship in the Lord Jesus Christ. They have opened themselves up to being baptized in the Holy Spirit. They are open to all the charismata revealed in the Scriptures and they are growing closer together in committed relationships. Yet they also had to obey the disciplines against intercommunion.

"So, what did they do? They decided that when the Catholic children made their first Holy Communion little Kenneth Twitchell would be assigned a very special place in the sanctuary. He would be present in an attitude of petition and intercession and supplication, praying that God would give our churches wisdom to end even the eucharistic disunity that we now experience."

Bertolucci explained that the following week young Twitchell made his Communion in his Presbyterian church. All the youngsters from the first Communion class in the Catholic church went to the Presbyterian church, dressed in their Sunday best, and had a special place in the Presbyterian sanctuary. They also interceded and prayed for the unity of the Body of Christ.

When Tom Twitchell related his story to the panel in Atlantic City, members of the panel began to cry. Bertolucci went to the microphone and told the some two thousand people assembled for the workshop, "Cry, brothers and sisters. Mourn. God's Spirit is here and is telling us not to praise right now; not to give thanks but to mourn and cry."

After relating the story, Bertolucci appealed to the stadium audience to walk down the road hand in hand, crying out to a nonbelieving world that *Jesus is Lord*. He said that he had an experience when he first became involved in the charismatic movement. A group of lay people prayed him into the Baptism in the Holy Spirit. He emphasized there's nothing more gorgeous than a group of lay people praying their clergy into the Baptism.

He asked the audience how many of them wanted their clergy to know what they were experiencing in the stadium. How many wanted the day to come when they all could share at the same Lord's Supper? How many wanted everyone in their churches and parishes and congregations to experience a personal Pentecost? He said the answer was in Matthew 18:19-20, which reads, "Again I tell you, if two of you join your voices on earth to pray for anything whatever, it shall be granted you by my Father in heaven. Where two or three are gathered in my name, there am I in their midst" (NAB).

"Hey!" exclaimed Bertolucci. "Look how many we have here today. See how the Lord's presence is magnified here today. I'm asking you to stand on the Word of God at this point. I really believe what the verse says. Are you going to stand with me? All right, right now, let us agree on total unity in the Body of Christ. Right now. Agree. 'Father, let it be so, let it be so. Amen!'

"We have power in this place such as no church has ever had gathered together. Do you want every bishop, cardinal, deacon, presbyter, elder, pastor, minister baptized in the Holy Spirit? OK, let's go at it. Agree! Agree! Amen! Yes, Lord. Hallelujah! Send forth Your Spirit. Come Holy Ghost. Hallelujah! Thank You God. Come Holy Spirit. Agree. Do I hear you saying Amen? Hallelujah. Do you want the church to come alive like it did on that first Pentecost? Agree. Agree right now. Agree. Hallelujah. Thank You God. Yes, Lord. Hallelujah. Jesus. Jesus. Thank You God. Thank You God.

"You want our nation to be a Christian nation, a Christ-centered nation, do you want that? Do you know the power we have in this stadium to bring that about? Stand on Matthew 18:19 right now. We want a Christian nation. Let's agree. Let's agree. Hallelujah. Amen, God. Father in Jesus name. Hallelujah Jesus, Glory, Glory, Glory. We agree Lord. Christian communities all over the country. Hallelujah. We agree Lord. A whole new counterculture. Might I say that we are revolutionaries for Jesus Christ. Hallelujah. Glory glory, glory to Jesus. Thank You Jesus. Thank You Jesus. Thank You Jesus.

"Don't sit down yet. There's something more we've got to ask Daddy, and it is Daddy's living room we're in today. The family is gathered together today. Hallelujah. Thank You God. We've got to ask Daddy one more thing. Let's tap into the power right here. I tell you again, if two of you join your voices on earth to pray for anything whatever, it shall be granted you, by my Daddy, in heaven. Agreed? Agreed? Agreed? OK.

"Father, God, my Daddy, in the name of Jesus Christ, Your Son, we pray that Protestants, Catholics, Anglicans, Orthodox and nondenominationals will love one another, will lay down their lives for one another. Agreed? Agreed? Agreed. That all those who profess belief in Jesus Christ, as Lord, will truly love one another and be empowered to lay down their lives for one another. Agree. Agree. Amen. Amen. Hallelujah. You with me?

"There's one more biggy coming. Who's going to win this world for Jesus Christ?"

"We are," came a huge chorus from the audience.

"You got it. I'm so happy you said that. I'm looking at a mighty army of evangelizers. Hallelujah! Glory! O brothers and sisters, you are the ones. I am the one. We are the ones. Don't just look down here on the stage. Don't think it's just going to be done through television. Don't think it's going to happen just through anointed preaching and teaching. I'm looking at you, the masses of God's people, who in a few minutes are going to go out there on the highways and byways and I'm going to stand on this Word right now. Hear it, hear it on the eve of Pentecost.

"On the vigil of Pentecost hear this Word. You will receive power when the Holy Spirit comes upon you. Then you are to be my witnesses. Here we are. We are the ones, as expressed in Acts 1:14. Don't you sit down yet. Together they devoted themselves to constant prayer. There were some women in their company, Mary, the mother of Jesus, and his brothers. Brothers and sisters, I believe the whole heavenly host of witnesses is all around us today.

"Now I'm asking you to stand on that Word and to ask right now for the coming of the Holy Spirit upon every individual in this assembly. Right now. Ask. Let every voice ask. Come Holy Spirit. Come Holy Spirit. Come

Holy Spirit. 'When the day of Pentecost came it found them gathered in one place. Suddenly from up in the sky there came a noise like a strong, driving wind which was heard all through the house where they were seated. Tongues as of fire appeared, which parted and came to rest on each of them. All were filled with the Holy Spirit. They began to express themselves in foreign tongues and make bold proclamations as the Spirit prompted them' (Acts 2:1-4 NAB).

"If the music ministry could just lead us in 'Spirit of the Living God,' then I'll resume some more thoughts but right now this is a precious moment. A precious moment. Stand on Matthew 18:19. Stand on the Word of God in Acts of the Apostles. Let that breath of the Holy Spirit come forth upon us to empower us to go forth and to be witnesses."

The audience sang, "Spirit of the Living God."

"Thank You Jesus! I want to conclude this sharing by outlining for you briefly, before we return to prayer and praise, what I regard as the seven C's. The *seven C's of success* on the *road to unity*." Father Bertolucci listed *number one* as *Communion*. He said, "First and foremost *is communion with the Lord Jesus Christ*. I pray that every single one of you in this stadium, you kids who are sitting way up there, you adults, you middle-aged persons, and you senior citizens, that you will each fall in love with the Lord Jesus Christ. That must be the first step. That you give your life to Him. That you surrender to Him. That you personally accept Him as your Lord and your God and your personal Savior. Are you ready to do that if you haven't already done it? Have you already done it? Then recommit yourself to Him. Pray for the day when we can share in the Holy Communion at the same table.

"But also, brothers and sisters, Protestants, Anglicans, Orthodox, Catholic, nondenominationals: *communion with one another*. Be united with one another. A Protestant stewardess on the plane and I prayed together on my way here. We both said when we finished that we were better persons in Christ for having prayed together. We had taken another step in growth in Christ.

" 'Beloved, let us love one another.' Now I'm here to tell you that is not an option any more. That is a commandment. And if you really love the Lord Jesus Christ, any of you who profess belief in Jesus as Lord, you are commanded by the Master who has given you salvation to love the person next to you who may be from another church. And part of that love, brothers and sisters, is forgiveness. Are you ready to wash one another's feet? We cannot yet share at the same Communion table, but we could have services of washing one another's feet, and we ought to do that. That could be a very creative way of expressing the unity we now have. Let's look at what we already have and build upon it.

"I made a retreat once with a Pentecostal minister of an independent church and an Episcopal priest. We'd go out on the beach in Maine, and we'd talk about our differences and we found out we weren't so different after all.

"That's what the second *C* is. Look at it on the scoreboard; what does it say? *Communication*. The second *C* is communication. You've got to talk to one another. The three of us would share our different theologies, our different ideas about salvation, our different ideas about the Holy Spirit, and then we'd talk about the different ways we could cooperate to evangelize.

"During the day we talked about the theory, and at night we put it into practice. When the sun set, we'd get into sports clothes, go onto the boardwalk area, on the oceanfront in Maine, and we'd walk up and down the street evangelizing. I'd never done that before. It's fun, walking up to people and saying, 'Could I share with you what the Lord Jesus Christ has done in my life?' And, you know, one of the fish we hooked there on the boardwalk was a fallen-away Roman Catholic.

"First the Pentecostal minister walked up to him and asked him a few questions. I was in the back with the Episcopal priest supporting him with prayer. The Pentecostal minister came back and said, 'John, he's one of yours, go after him.' So I went after him. We started walking along and the other two, the Pentecostal and the Episcopalian, were backing me up with prayer. All of a sudden, as we were walking along, we came to a coffee shop. I walked in, and I asked the man, 'May we stop in here?' He said, 'Yes, this is a Christian coffee shop and I am a Baptist pastor.' I said, 'Glory be to God, now we've got a Baptist in on the whole thing.'

"*Cooperation* and *Collaboration*. See those *other two C's* on the scoreboard. You know what happened within three hours. I, a Roman Catholic, heard his confession. The Baptist minister gave an altar call that brought him to the Lord Jesus Christ personally. The Episcopal priest took a deep concern about making sure he was under the right church authority, and the Pentecostal laid hands on him and got him baptized in the Holy Spirit. Now *that's cooperation* and *collaboration.*

"Then there's *Consideration.* Brothers and sisters, be considerate of one another. You know what it says in 1 Peter. 'Venerate the Lord that is Christ in your hearts.' Should anyone ask you the reason for this hope of yours be ever ready to reply, but speak gently and respectfully. Be considerate of each one's knowledge and understanding. Understand my position on Mary. Don't criticize it until you understand it, and don't criticize it even when you understand it. I don't ask you to agree. I ask you to understand why I submit to the Cardinal and to the Archbishop. Be considerate of where each one of us is at.

"And the *next C* is *Continuation.* It means *constancy,* and what it really means is 'hang in there.' 'Hang in there' with the crucified and risen Christ Jesus. 'Hang in there' when the going gets rough. 'Hang in there' when they persecute you. 'Hang in there' when they call you holy rollers. 'Hang in there' when they say you're fanatic. 'Hang in there' when they think you've flipped your lid. 'Hang in there' with the crucified and risen Lord Jesus Christ.

"And finally, brothers and sisters, *Celebration.* You already know what that's about. Learn how to praise the Lord, to sing and to raise your hands and to have a good time. Celebrate! Celebrate! Because the victory is already won. Celebrate for He is here. He is risen and He is sending forth His Holy Spirit. He is here. The Prince of peace. Mighty God! The wonderful Counselor! The Holy One! The Lamb of God! The Prince of Light! The Lord

God Almighty! The Lion of the Tribe of Judah! The Root of David! The Lord of Life! The Author and Finisher of our Faith! The Advocate! The Way! The Dayspring! The Lord of All! The Lamb! The Son of God! The Shepherd! The Messiah! The Truth! The Savior! The Chief Cornerstone! The Righteous Judge! The Light of the World! The Head of the Church! The Morningstar! The Star of Righteousness! The Chief Shepherd! The Resurrection and the Life! The Horn of Salvation! The Governor! The Alpha and Omega! The Lord of Lords and the King of Kings is here!"

Bertolucci closed his message with the audience singing "How Great Thou Art."

CHAPTER 12

The Clergy Reflect on Jesus 78

Many of the clergy who attended Jesus 78 in Giants' Stadium, some with members of their churches and parishes, have written their impressions which reflect an enthusiasm for additional such rallies and a gratefulness for the deep spiritual experience.

The Reverend Allen A. Ruscito, associate pastor of the First Presbyterian Church, Dunellen, New Jersey wrote: "Jesus 78 was a Celebration of Joy. In some ways it is hard to describe. It was more than a rally or a crusade. It was something of a festival of happiness—flowing from hearts filled with rivers of living waters. Those who came represented the whole Body of Christ—Protestant, Catholic, black, white, Oriental, men, women, rich, poor, young, old, healthy and sick. They came in buses, cars, vans. They came with Bibles, banners, guitars, tambourines and knapsacks. It was like a family reunion of the separated people of God coming together, welcoming each other and loving each other in the Lord.

"But it was much more than a gathering of people with

common religious interests. It was a daylong service of praise, prayer and proclamation of God—Father, Son and Holy Spirit—in which His name was magnified for all His mighty works in our lives. Jesus the Lord was gloriously proclaimed as victor over all the powers of darkness and destruction and as the Father's answer to the problems and needs of the world.

"The event was a genuine expression and experience of spiritual ecumenism in which God's people came together to affirm their oneness in Christ and to express that oneness in worship and word. The atmosphere was charged with a sense of the presence and power of God. The spirit was one of intense and genuine devotion from the moment we entered to the lovely strains of the ancient Catholic hymn, 'Holy God We Praise Thy Name,' to near the conclusion when we joined together in the great Protestant hymn, 'How Great Thou Art.'

"It seemed that what church councils, theological consultations and joint task forces strive so nobly to achieve was accomplished almost, as it were, instantaneously—a unity of spirit and intention, an openness to each other in Christian love and a desire to work together for the Kingdom of Christ to the glory of God. Jesus 78 demonstrated that the barriers that separate Christians can be transcended genuinely without blithely or irresponsibly obliterating our convictions or distinctive characteristics. It demonstrated both the unity and diversity of the Body of Christ in a loving, dynamic way.

"Finally Jesus 78 was a sign of hope to our world, a promise of the coming of God's reign in our day, a token of

God's love to His people everywhere. It was both a pronouncement of God's intention to heal the divisions and brokenness of His people and a plea to Him to fulfill His promises speedily. It was a reminder that redemption at heart is holistic, that God wants to redeem the whole person and His whole society and that salvation includes the healing and renewal of all the fractures and wounds of man and his world.

"Jesus 78 attempted to tell the church and the world that these desires were not the elusive dreams of visionaries, but were indeed a reality by the power of the Holy Spirit who has given to God's people to apply Christ's redemption, to fulfill the Father's purposes and to equip His people to serve Him in the world."

Father Michael Scanlan, president of the College of Steubenville in Ohio and one of the principal speakers at Jesus 78, wrote in his reflections of that eventful day for the glory of Jesus Christ:

"Jesus 78 was a unique moment in my life. It was a life-changing experience, not because of the large crowd which was impressive, not because of the great praise and song, not because of the prayerful men and women of God who testified and preached but because of what God did in me. I experienced a call to pray, preach, teach, love and work for the Body of Christ as the central reality of my life. This is so because I have come to believe that the unity of the Body of Christ is the first priority in God's heart and God is making it the first priority in mine.

"This was not the result of specific experiences or teaching. It was simply a grace from God as I prayed in

Giants' Stadium on the Vigil of Pentecost. I saw clearly that Jesus died and rose as the way of redemption so that the Body of Christ could live forever. I saw that the great miracle of Pentecost is to be the unity of Christians and that the Pentecost miracle is to be the great sign to the world that the Father sent Jesus and that we are loved by the Father in the same way that He loves Jesus. This is so overwhelmingly clear in the teaching of John 17:20-23:

" 'I do not pray for them alone. I pray also for those who will believe in me through their word, that all may be one as you, Father, are in me, and I in you; I pray that they may be [one] in us, that the world may believe that you sent me. I have given them the glory you gave me that they may be one, as we are one—I living in them, you living in me—that their unity may be complete. So shall the world know that you sent me, and that you loved them as you loved me' (NAB).

"Suddenly, years of agonizing over problems of families, hunger, persecution, racism and loneliness, indeed all the world's problems, came to focus in the realization that the only permanent solution is to be incorporated in the Body of Christ. Marriage will only be successful when supported by the Body of Christ, children will only get the full teaching and love they need through the care of many members of the Body of Christ, the poor and the sick of the world will only get their needs fully met by the pooled resources of the Body of Christ. In fact where there is unity of brothers and sisters there are no problems that cannot be resolved.

"The Body of Christ will remain forever. As I experienced God's grace and looked at the 60,000 present praying in the Spirit, I knew that the Body of Christ was the answer and that I would henceforth be different. My life would be given for the Body of Christ."

The Reverend Donald K. Theobald, pastor of the Presbyterian Church in Harrison, New York, found Jesus 78 reminding him of experiences from out of the past and promises for the future. He reported:

" 'Jesus Christ is Lord' expressed the uniting concept that brought more than 50,000 praising and singing followers to the Meadowlands. Could it happen in the New York City area? It did—praise God. All gathered to praise God for the great gift of His Son, to pray as did Jesus 'that they may be one' and to share the powerful presence of God, the Holy Spirit.

"Sitting there I remembered that first announcement in the mail. It was autumn and the leaves were falling. May 13, 1978. Mark the calendar—the day before Pentecost, the day before the twenty-second anniversary of my installation in my present pastorate, the day before Mother's Day and the day before my birthday. It had been easy to remember. A day of wonderful preparation for Pentecost Sunday. Truly this is a sign that the Holy Spirit is opening a new era for the children of God. One in Spirit, praising the God of salvation and united under the banner 'Jesus Christ is Lord.'

"Thoughts of the passing months with prayers and more prayers, planning and finally the leap of faith in hiring a fifty-passenger bus. Would it be filled? Almost immediately every seat was reserved. More prayer and it was 6:30 A.M. May 13th.

"With that overcast sky and threat of rain I prayed

PROPHECY IN ACTION

'Lord, why?' Doubt in my heart was confirmed by the parade of raincoats and umbrellas that accompanied those who boarded the bus. 'I had a dream last night,' reported Kathy, 'I saw a rainbow over the stadium. It's not going to rain.' Song began to fill the bus. Presbyterians, Baptists, Roman Catholics, and Pentecostals sang. Norm Sherry gave a word of personal testimony and all joined in praise to the Lord. As we left the parking area and moved to our seats, an excitement of His being there filled the group, both young and old alike.

"Arriving early, we were surprised to see the two lower levels of the stadium almost filled. Soon a Roman Catholic priest called the thousands to join in singing praise to God, to Jesus and to the Holy Spirit.

"The power of Christian love was manifest in attitude, in touching and in sharing. Proper persons raised their hands in praise to God while Pentecostals danced before the Lord. People of all races and stations of life clapped their hands in unity. The morning passed quickly and it was lunch time. It was like a great family sharing conversation and food. In front of us was a Roman Catholic group from Lancaster, Pennsylvania who thoughtfully invited a Protestant recently widowed to come with them, praying that the event would help lift her burden of loneliness.

"It was during the lunch time that I started praising God for the overcast weather. If the May sun had been in full view many would have been extremely uncomfortable and some might have become ill. 'The Cloud by Day' was the assurance of God's being with the Israelites in the Sinai Desert. Now the 'greater than Moses' was showing to us that new assurance of God's presence in the New Jersey Meadowlands, The Fire of the Holy Spirit.

"I was awed by the sensitivity of the president's sister in presenting the healing power for the whole man available in Jesus and Jesus alone. Praise the Lord Club's Jim Bakker dramatically emphasized the New Commandment of Jesus, 'to love one another.' God had spoken to him in his hour of confusion, 'Jim, you love them, I will judge them.' The Holy Spirit was speaking to me and to others. Just prior to Jim's message a problem arose that would have ruined the bus trip home. A judgmental problem to which I could see no answer. 'Let us pray about it.' After the message the problem was solved in true Christian love. The trip home was one of real love and fellowship in the Holy Spirit.

"As a Presbyterian minister in a Roman Catholic town, the closing message by Father Bertolucci hit close to my heart. Especially the illustration about Communion and Confirmation with the Catholic youth and the Presbyterian minister's son and his call to make Jesus Lord and when that is done all man-made walls and barriers will crumble away. They were crumbling that day.

"What a day! How much more meaningful was Pentecost in the year of our Lord 1978."

The Reverend Father George B. Murphy, S.J., of the Loyola House of Retreats in Morristown, New Jersey did not attend the Jesus 78 Rally as a charismatic. He brought a friend whom he called Harvey and he emphasized that he came to give God one full day of praise for Him and His

Holy Name. He reported:

"Harvey and I took off in the early morning under clouds that promised a great deal of rain. The gusty winds took away what little hope we had for good weather. In about forty minutes we were part of a growing stream of cars following the long curving approaches to the stadium parking areas. Window decals, bumper stickers and hand lettered signs all gave clues to our common destination. Crowds of cars gave place to crowds of people as we walked to the stadium entrance gates, went up the escalators onto the ramps and then to our seats! Forty minutes ahead of time and already a large crowd had assembled. Hands were waving, signs swung back and forth and voices called out to attract the newly arrived. We were hardly seated before we sensed one great feeling—everyone was happy to be there and they didn't hesitate to show it!

"The day's program began promptly. From that moment on so efficiently did things move that all you sensed was smoothness. Speakers gave their messages and stirred and lifted us. Groups sang and we all sang; English or Spanish it mattered little. For that day we were all linguists. There was a treasure trove of things to wonder at. The laden skies that threatened but dropped not a drop of rain. The chill wind that brought only sounds across the stadium. The giant scoreboards that flashed the praises of God all through the day with wonderful variety and ingenuity. The folk groups who sang to us and who had us joining them by the time the second chorus came around. Can you imagine a background of 60,000 voices?

"I want to share with you a few moments that were all

mine—quiet, deep moments which moved me greatly. Those moments will be with me for a long time. I have used them in talking to others and in my homilies. I am grateful to God for them and hope you will enjoy reading about them.

"What transpired was this. In the afternoon I was sweeping the rows of seats with a pair of field glasses when I noticed that one whole section was not looking at the speaker. Instead the eyes of the people in that section were watching intently the figure of a man who had his back to the speaker! It quickly dawned on me what this was. The solitary figure was a 'signer.' He was repeating in sign language to the group before him the words of the speaker. The group in front of him were all deaf-mutes. In that vast stadium, full of song, joyful laughter, happy voices, suddenly there was this pocket of silence. Sound was all that was missing. As my glasses swept the faces of that area I could easily detect the joy, happiness, the interior laughter—it was all there. Nothing was really missing. As I continued to watch, they 'sang' with their hands one of the hymns with which the rest of the people in the stadium were using their voices to praise God.

"Time and again my eyes went back to that group. Harvey and I both watched. After a time I noticed that there were different 'signers.' They were spelling one another. No matter who signed, however, the attention was the same. You could almost feel the intensity. Then it hit me! That signer was the most important person in the stadium for the speakers as well as for those to whom she or he was signing. Everything depended on the signer's mind. Whatever it absorbed of the speaker's message would be transmitted. Suppose there was prejudice there? Suppose there was indifference there? Suppose there was lack of understanding? What was heard was heard by one person alone. What was 'listened to' was 'listened to' by hundreds. Everyone of those hundreds depended on that signer! He or she was a powerful person—for good or evil.

"I was fascinated and I stared. Gradually this thought began to blossom in my mind: as a priest, how much does God depend on me to get His message to others. How much, too, do those I counsel, preach to or teach depend on me. I am the signer! God, knowing me and my limitations still chooses me. Those who hear me know they are listening to a man of limitations and still they listen time and again. From God and from my people a great vote of confidence and not blindly given! There is deep responsibility to be a 'signer' of God's Word but its a joyful task when you consider the understanding and acceptance that surround you.

"I enjoyed the day very much and it also proved to be very profitable when it comes to comprehending my priestly vocation.

"One more remembrance and this is on the light side. As Harvey and I left the stadium, we were deep in conversation about the day, its events, the old friends we met. We didn't notice but we exited through the wrong gates. We were lost and so was our car. Forty minutes later we found the right parking lot and there was the Nova sitting in solitary splendor. As we got into the car, Harvey looked across the top of the car and suggested we go back into the stadium and ask for a healing of memories. I said, 'That's not the healing they were speaking about, Harvey!' And so back home."

Although not an ordained minister, Mrs. Ruth Stapleton's reflections are included with the clergy because she does have an inner healing ministry and is much in demand as a speaker at Christian gatherings. She writes:

"Jesus 78: It was a time for a wonderful outpouring of the Holy Spirit. I was certainly very honored to be a part of this celebration where praises in word and song were lifted in the name of Jesus Christ. Gatherings such as Jesus 78 are very important because as we come together—thousands of believers—we are making a statement to the entire world. We are saying, 'Yes, there is a way to make our lives meaningful, there is hope, there is a source of eternal love and strength. There is a way in which wholeness can be brought to the broken of this world.'

"You see, Jesus Christ wants us all to be whole, complete persons. He wants us all to live abundant lives. He has a perfect plan for each of our lives, and we can know and realize that plan if we will only trust Him, and follow Him each day. Jesus 78: a time of praise, a spiritual awakening, renewed strength and energy to return to our places of service and do the work He has for us; a time of fun and fellowship . . . a statement to the world saying, 'Yes, it can work, we can live abundant lives . . . through Him.'

"I received a special blessing from Jesus 78 and I am happy to have been a part of the gathering of believers."

PROPHECY IN ACTION

The Reverend Dr. Robert C. Woodward, pastor of Trinity Evangelical Congregational Church, Palmerton, Pennsylvania, is the four-year ecumenical observer for all charismatic meetings, representing the Evangelical Congregational church. He found the Spirit of God and Christ present as persons in Giants' Stadium. He was touched by the "silent harmony and praying by the thousands present which was outdone only by the gladsome harmony of the Holy Spirit as He too stamped His approval on our being one with Him."

Dr. Woodward continued: "I didn't know what to expect but everything went along so smoothly. I could feel the presence of the Holy Spirit. The comradeship between the Protestants and Catholics was exceptionally exciting and gratifying. I found in the charismatic movement a unity in the Body of Jesus Christ that does not exist anywhere else.

"Now I am looking forward to the next great rally since at Jesus 78 I found all the speakers spiritually exhilarating and the responses from the audience as Jesus had commanded: 'Love one another as I have loved you.' I wish every Christian could have attended Jesus 78 because they would have come away, as did so many in attendance, changed personalities. They were changed because they found the presence of the Holy Spirit in a new and profound way."

Dr. Woodward stated that he experienced a miraculous healing from a heart attack a few years ago.

The Reverend G. Milton Johnson, pastor of

Gethsemane Lutheran Church in Plainfield, New Jersey, saw Jesus 78 as a wedding with the focus on the bridegroom. The rally brought back other memories of visits to the stadium as he relates in the following letter: "I had been at Giants' Stadium in the Meadowlands many times to see the Cosmos play soccer. I had seen the stadium packed with spectators watching Pelé play. I had been there when Pelé played his farewell game. The day he led the crowd in shouting the word 'love.' I had come again to Giants' Stadium on the Saturday before Pentecost. The crowd was there, just as before, but with a difference. These were Christians come together to praise and worship the Lord Jesus. Pelé's word 'love' now received a name, 'Jesus.'

"I remember thinking as we got off the bus at the Meadowlands, 'If nothing else happened today, all these people coming together was significant enough in itself.' It was amazing to see the people coming into a sports stadium to worship the Lord Jesus Christ. It was the people who were there that made the day for me. Jim Bakker's description was an apt one, it was a 'wedding rehearsal.' The many members of the family who were going to be united were getting together to know each other before the wedding.

"Still the focus was on the bridegroom. It was our eyes fixed on Jesus that lifted our vision above the walls that separated. I felt we had a taste of what that oneness will be that Jesus prayed about in the seventeenth chapter of the Gospel of St. John: 'I pray that they may all be one, Father. May they be one, so that the world will believe that you sent me' (TEV).

"It was only a taste however, because we all had to return to where we had come from. I felt there was a sense of caution that we could not leave our denominational structures, for the building of unity is not yet complete. Our various points of view and historical developments are the scaffolding for the yet uncompleted body of the church.

"Yet the joy and the love is already there. We saw it that Saturday, as people hugged one another. We were strangers yet it didn't seem to matter. That day we knew we were brothers and sisters.

"It was evident in the singing too. Some of us didn't know all of the songs but tried anyway. We learned and were eager to be a part of it all. Many of us tried to sing in Spanish because we felt a closeness to all who were there. When the familiar songs were sung and praise lifted to the heavens you could feel the bond of the Spirit of God. When we sang in the Spirit it was as if heavens had come to earth. Jesus was with us and we were with Him.

"There were individual responses by members of our congregation to what was happening. One of our deacons who had been a Roman Catholic and had some unhappy experiences as a child found a sense of reconciliation as he hugged some Roman Catholic sisters who were seated near him. One of our women had an experience of the Holy Spirit during the praise and worship.

"All of our people were very moved by Father Bertolucci and his message. We also felt that the Lord gave us a sign of His confirmation of the day. That sign came as the sun parted the clouds that had been over the stadium all day, as we stood in agreement in our prayers for unity, led by Father Bertolucci. It was as if the Lord was saying, 'It pleases me that my children have come together in my name.'

"I felt the day could have gone on and on. It was a moment of joy that whetted my appetite for more. I feel that the Lord is really calling His people together and Jesus 78 was an evidence of it. I feel too that it will be the witness of our unity that will cause the world to be more open to the message of Jesus as Lord."

The Reverend Dean H. Whitney has served four parishes in Iowa, Illinois and Staten Island and Brooklyn in New York state. He presently is Metropolitan New York Area Director for "The 700 Club" of the Christian Broadcasting Network. Reverend Whitney writes:

"Any time you get 60,000 people together for a whole day to hear the Word of God and to praise the Lord, that's significant! And when the group includes Catholics, Protestants, Jewish Christians, blacks, whites, Hispanics, and almost any other background imaginable, that's more significant! But when the news media reports the event so well without open ridicule or criticism, then you know God has done something of historic significance!

"There was *so* much of great importance about that day at the Meadowlands. But *three* aspects of the event stood out in my mind. First, as I watched the scoreboards flash 'Jesus . . . Jesus . . . JESUS' and 'Hallelujah!' I thrilled to the fact that there in a secular stadium on a playing field, built to display the achievements of men, *the Lordship of Jesus Christ* was being even more demonstrated than spoken.

"It wasn't until I woke the next day with a slight sunburn that I realized that this Lord had exercised lordship over the weather not only in opening the clouds late in the afternoon as we chanted His praise, but also in sheltering us the rest of the day from the blistering power of the sun. How very essential it is for the Body of Christ today to believe that He is LORD! . . . that He is not wringing His hands in frustration over the circumstances of this world, but that He is Lord; and that we are not adherents of a religion largely ignored by the world but that we are the army, the very Body of the Lord of lords, and King of kings. In the Church today vision is crucial . . . vision of who Jesus really is, vision of who we really are, and vision of what He can do and is doing through us.

"Second, I was impressed by the *revolution of love, trust* and *unity* that is taking place in the Body of Christ! Almost unbelievable movement has come in the past ten years toward melting the hostilities that existed between Catholics and Protestants and among Protestants of different backgrounds. I almost had to pinch myself from time to time in order to grasp what was really happening as we hugged, sang, worshiped, listened, and shouted praise whether the person at the microphone was a Catholic archbishop, a Pentecostal preacher, or a black gospel singer. Whether we comprehend it or not, this is a change of revolutionary dimensions toward the fulfillment of Jesus' prayer for oneness among His people.

"Finally, I was especially pleased that this first gathering of its kind happened in the New York metropolitan area. Too many people are inclined to give up on this city . . . but the devil hasn't, and praise the Lord neither has almighty God! This city influences the thinking, the values and the life style of the rest of the world more than any other city. Let's claim it as a place for GOD'S GLORY now!"

In reflecting on Jesus 78, Father Jack Martin, a member of the team ministry at St. Ann's Roman Catholic Church in Newark, New Jersey, found that by some people's definition he is not full-fledged "into the charismatic." He asserts that "For me, the acid test is the fruit borne. So, 'outsider,' though I may be classified, I saw evidence of God's presence and mysterious action that chilly day in May.

"Our contingent was a mixed gathering, if ever there was one. We had fifteen-year-olds and those in their seventies. We were black and white, Catholic and non-Catholic, Hispanic and part-Indian, religious and laity. Sitting at my side, sharing our blankets and hot coffee (as well as our 'praise God' and 'Alabaré') were a black teen-age young man and a Puerto Rican grandmother. (We had all kinds of categories in our group, except 'rich.') It seemed as though, by God's design, like the deaf who were being signed translation, all our people were hearing 'each in his own tongue' the message about Jesus and His Good Spirit.

"Our gospel choir sings the moving hymn, 'To the Utmost, Jesus Saves.' When the great gospel singer, Rev. James Cleveland, introduces that hymn on one of his record albums, he says, 'We can brag tonight because our God is *able*. And I'm here to tell you, He'll be for you whatever you let Him be.'

"I saw God being what our mosaic of central Newarkers

let Him be. We were all poor, but we went home enriched in our hearts. The day was one of healing and deepening for our gathering of believers in Jesus."

Father Paul Viale of Christ the King Roman Catholic Church in Jersey City, New Jersey, believes that some people missed the historical significance of Jesus 78. He asks "How did it happen?" He goes on to develop an explanation, writing that just thirteen years after the end of the second Vatican Council, more than 60,000 Catholics and Protestants assemble under co-sponsorship to worship the Father, listen to each others' speakers, and get an inkling of Christian unity. The Spirit who took us this far isn't tired and yet some of us are just learning that something has been missing.

"I'm glad that this significant, ecumenical step in the metropolitan area happened in our archdiocese. I believe we have the potential to follow through so that we will not fall into the early pattern of the ecumenical movement of just celebrating together on Thanksgiving Day and being satisfied with the dormant relationship the rest of the year.

"Some people experienced Jesus 78 as an isolated demonstration but missed the historical significance of what is happening in the Body of Christ. It almost seems that we cannot realize the value and necessity of internal, spiritual and demonstrated unity until we know how much our divisions are heavy upon the heart of Christ. His desire and prayer for oneness among his followers is all the motivation we need. The Vatican II documents made it official and public—now all we need is the 'local vision' the Lord will give those who ask for it."

CHAPTER 13

The People Are the Prophecy

The Friday evening preceding the Jesus 78 Rally the planning committee had gathered to wrap up the final plans. They were discussing the number of people who could be expected and the prophecies that had been made concerning the rally. Jim Ferry suddenly repeated the prophecy given earlier in the in the evening by Fr. Bill O'Brien, "The people are the prophecy." He continued, "They are the ones who will make it a success as they are directed by the Holy Spirit."

It was decided then that, since the people are the prophecy, those attending would be asked to write their impressions. The response was gratifying. Regrettably, not all the letters received could be published because of space limitations. Those which were omitted did not lack in quality. The ones published are representative testimonies of the blessings received at Jesus 78.

John Wesley and many noted personages were influenced through their mother's love and teachings. The year of Jesus 78, Mother's Day came on May 14, the same day as Pentecost Sunday, the day following the rally. It led Joseph C. Kelly of Elmhurst, New York to note, "Mother's Love is a Blessing." He wrote the following: "My mother asked all her family to join her for Jesus 78. At that time I was a sinner. I had not thought much about God in the past twenty years. Love for my mother and mindful of all the sacrifices she had made for her family, I happily decided that my wife and I would go with mother. So did my brother and all my sisters. Praise the Lord!

"I cannot explain the wonderful feeling of relief I received that day. I know now that it was the Holy Spirit that entered my body and soul and gave me that relief and happiness. I raised my hands to the Lord and asked forgiveness for my past sins. I was born again in Jesus. I am happy to say so was my wife, and wonderful things have been happening to our family since.

"While I was writing this letter, my youngest son, eight years old, came to me and said again that he wants to be a priest. I know the Lord is blessing my family."

In 2 Peter 3:9, the Scripture tells us that "The Lord is not willing that any should perish." The following letter from Susan Kane, Kingston, Pennsylvania, and others tell of people who were saved at Jesus 78.

"Jesus 78 was the first wonderful experience since giving my heart to the Lord in 1971. I attended with my parents and some friends. It seemed that heaven was opening during the time of agreeing and praying with Father Bertolucci. I prayed with all my heart for the Holy Spirit to save everyone in our household.

"While I was praying in the stadium, my husband at home woke up with such a peace in his heart. The next day, the Day of Pentecost, he gave his heart to the Lord. I know our entire household will be saved. Praise the Lord!"

Mrs. Janet Grosso of New York City attended Jesus 78 with her mother. Both had been baptized with the Holy Spirit. She explained, "My husband and brother are Catholic but did not know anything about the charismatic movement. Neither did they want to attend the rally. When Father Bertolucci spoke, however, my brother was completely moved and started raising his hands and praising the Lord."

Marie Parfinick of Nutley, New Jersey wrote that she had been attending the Holy Family Prayer Group with a friend for three years. She confides, "My husband and family thought I had joined some crazy Holy Roller church. I prayed for all of them.

"Last year my husband turned to Jesus when he came up against some trouble in his life. Now he is baptized in the Spirit and came to Jesus 78. He is now drunk in the Holy Spirit. Praise the Lord!"

The twenty-year-old son of Mrs. Mary De Temple of Orangeburg, New York, a little league coach, was excited about attending Jesus 78, but was prevented from coming the last minute because he could not get another coach to replace him in a scheduled game. She related, "I told him not to feel bad. I was sure the Lord was going to use the ticket for someone who needed Jesus more than he did at this time. That morning about five o'clock a friend called to ask if I had an extra ticket for her husband who wasn't in the Lord. Praise the Lord, he went." Mrs. De Temple is a member of St. Anthony's prayer group in Orangeburg.

PROPHECY IN ACTION

And this exciting letter from Marvin Federman, Nutley, New Jersey: "I was born into the Hebrew faith but never practiced my religion. For years I lived only by the Ten Commandments. I read books about Christ but never was convinced until I read a book this past January that made me a believer. My new discovery was exciting. I now attend a church weekly and took off from work to come to Jesus 78.

"It was extremely fascinating and rewarding to me and my wife. Never did I witness so many people proclaiming their love and devotion to anyone, including Jesus. We have a lot in common with others now. The charismatic movement is wonderful. It has helped me to become deeper involved in my new religion and in Christ."

A Croydon, Pennsylvania resident, John A. Boston admits that before Jesus 78, he hadn't been to church in twenty years. But a friend of his had an extra ticket for the rally, so he decided to go "for the prime reason of a day's outing." His friend said, "It was in the hands of the Lord."

"I was a little bored in the morning," relates Boston. "But something happened to me in the afternoon. I looked at all the faces around me and wanted what they had. I started back to church, joined a charismatic prayer group, was baptized in the Holy Spirit and haven't felt such peace in years. Praise God!"

The Holy Spirit seemed to touch everyone in some way. Many told of inner healings, forgiveness and rededication in their lives. A woman from the First Presbyterian Church in Green Lawn, New York reported, "I went to Jesus 78 just to praise the Lord and be with God's people.

The People Are the Prophecy

When I returned home I felt differently, especially towards my husband. It wasn't until five days later while talking with my friends, during our 'The Arts for Christ' session, that I realized Jesus had given me an inner healing concerning my husband.

"He is an alcoholic and he has hurt me very deeply many times. It had gotten so I couldn't really love him any more. But Jesus healed me. I am able now to forgive him and love him dearly."

A Rahway, New Jersey resident and member of the Grace and Peace Fellowship Church, Jolinn M. Twaskas witnessed a miracle. "Jesus 78 was the first event of its kind in which I had participated. I wasn't sure what to expect. My husband is a very shy person and never sings or prays aloud at our weekly services.

"At the rally he said he wanted to, and almost did join in song. Afterward he was totally committed to the Lord. He has been an alcoholic for over seven years and had been in a rehabilitation home for alcoholics three weeks prior to coming to Jesus 78. Now he is a new man. The Lord is really working in our lives. Praise God."

From Alan Temple, Poughkeepsie, New York: "The main reason I went to Jesus 78 was to keep some younger brothers and sisters company. Jesus had a different reason. Much of the year '78 had been confusion for me. I did not know where I was going and why the Lord had seen fit to bless me with certain trials.

"From the people in my home church to those I hang around with, I seemed only to pick out the bad points in people's lives. I was blessed through teaching of Jim Bakker when he said the Lord told him, 'You love them and I'll judge them.' God began healing my attitude that day. Since then Jesus has been trying to perfect me in this area. Thank You Jesus for people sensitive enough to needs to hold an event like Jesus 78. Praise Jesus!"

Mary Jo Poster of Brooklyn felt unwanted and out of place within her church. She was in a state of "I do not belong." She couldn't see an answer to her problem and in some degrees still cannot but she reported that one theme at the rally came across to her—"that individually as well as communally, we are all loved by an infinite God-man, Jesus Christ. We are children of a heavenly Father. I am trying to live what Jim Bakker said, 'You love them and I will judge them.' Thank you for sharing God's promises in Jesus 78." Mary Jo Poster is a member of the Good Shepherd Catholic Charismatic Prayer group in Poughkeepsie.

"Since hearing Father John Bertolucci's Spirit-filled message, a gentle, steady healing is occurring with me daily," stated Ramona Colao of the Union County Hope Center in New Jersey. "Also Jim Bakker's response from God, 'You do the loving and I'll do the judging,' was seared into my heart. With deep joy I now find that when I begin to judge, I immediately am aware of Christ whispering, 'Ramona, you do the loving, I'll do the judging.' What a radiant freedom this brings."

"I went to Jesus 78 alone and was sitting by myself when a girl, sitting with her family, asked me to join them. I was full of joy because the family had the love of Jesus. I've been a born-again Christian for three years but situations in life had brought me down, leaving me feeling alone and unloved. The feeling that I shared someone very special—Jesus—with everyone at the rally brought me closer to Him. The messages, prayers, singing and the family I was invited to join brought me back to the Cross where I knew I belonged. Thank You, Jesus!" exclaimed Siobhan Stevens of St. Matthews Trinity Lutheran Church, Hoboken, New Jersey.

"God is a Spirit, and they that worship him must worship him in spirit and in truth" (John 4:24).

Virtually all attending Jesus 78 were impressed with the love and friendliness shared with so many Christians of different denominations and churches as they praised, sang and exalted the Lord together.

Mrs. Yamile Stark of Morganville, New Jersey, and a member of St. Thomas More Church, found both gladness and a note of sadness at Jesus 78. "My heart was filled with gladness when we sang," she wrote. "I looked up to heaven and could practically see and hear the angels and archangels and all the choirs of heaven join us. I could also feel the communion of saints smiling and rejoicing with us.

"It was a day for the universe to tremble with emotion and excitement at being one with their Lord and Creator. The wonderful experience will stay with me forever.

"I am a Catholic but it would be nice if you could convince more Protestants to be speakers. Your emphasis on unity was great. Keep it up.

"The only sad note was that we could not receive Communion together."

John Durland, a member of the Calvary Assembly, Chester, New York, sent the following. "I am so thankful that the Holy Spirit led me to attend Jesus 78, and enjoy the day with other born-again Christians.

PROPHECY IN ACTION

"Christians are being stirred to serve God rather than church organizations, church structures, Catholic traditions and social standings in their communities. I praise God that this is coming to pass." Donna Pace of Westfield, New Jersey was amazed by the number of fellow Christians at Jesus 78. "We could feel the Spirit moving, and knew that God had great plans for all of us whatever denomination we were.

"It was a moving experience to see all those different people, all shapes and sizes, all types of personalities, all walks of life—all acting with one accord. I said to my friends, 'Just look at all those faces. Take a good look. When we all get to heaven, you'll be seeing the same faces.' "

From Harry S. Evans, Sr., a member of Koinonia Full Gospel Fellowship and a Mennonite prayer group in Telford, Pennsylvania came this statement: "Only the sweet, beautiful power of the Holy Spirit could unite people of so many different churches. I have been in large groups before where there was much unity in the family of God but anything as large as Jesus 78 staggered the imagination."

Brother Vince Paczkowski of Don Bosco College in Newton, New Jersey wrote that "Jesus 78 was a beautiful testimony of faith. The whole day of sharing God's presence with so many people of different faiths gave me encouragement and strength to live as a faithful follower of Jesus. It was an experience I will never forget.

"Just before Jesus 78 I was baptized in the Holy Spirit. This event by its beautiful testimony of faith strengthened me in the life of the Spirit."

The People Are the Prophecy

A Sussex, New Jersey resident, Ronald Wyka considered the coming together of many Spirit-filled Christians of different religious backgrounds—all lifting their voices to the Lord—the most beautiful aspect of Jesus 78. "It was so moving that the music, the speakers and the involvement of those attending gave me goose bumps at times."

Blessed tremendously were Frank Annese and his wife of East Meadow, New York. "It was beautiful getting people from different denominations together in one place at one time. It is living proof of how the Holy Spirit works in manifesting the love of Jesus. We were greatly moved by all the speakers and will be back for Jesus 79."

Some attending Jesus 78 had the confusion in their minds cleared after listening to the messages. This happened to Constance Amabili of Bristol, Pennsylvania, a member of Zion Lutheran Church and the Great Shepherd Prayer Community, a Catholic group. She wrote: "Riding in the bus on our way to Jesus 78 a conversation developed among six of us as to how I adjusted to being a member of a Lutheran Church after being raised Roman Catholic.

"I joined Zion Lutheran Church after ten years of being inactive as a church member and one year before receiving Jesus Christ as Savior. I told the people on the bus the problem was not in adjusting to my church but to the attitudes of many people about belonging to a Lutheran church and communing in a Catholic church with a Catholic prayer group. When we profess to be Christians, I cannot see why people of one denomination cannot commune in a church of another.

PROPHECY IN ACTION

"We left that conversation behind us as we entered the stadium and forgot about it until Father Bertolucci shared the beautiful story of the Presbyterian minister's son who was not allowed to receive his first Holy Communion with his Catholic classmates. As the Lord spoke through Father Bertolucci about our strife for unity, all the questions going through my mind were beautifully answered in less than two hours. Praise God!"

Especially impressed by both Ruth Stapleton and Father Bertolucci was Thomas J. Dolan, Jr., Silver Springs, Maryland. Mr. Dolan is a member of Catholic University Prayer Group in Washington, D.C. He found the speaking styles of Mrs. Stapleton and Father Bertolucci different while their message—Jesus is Lord—was the same.

Mr. Dolan related that listening to Mrs. Stapleton was like being in a small informal group in someone's home. She spoke quietly and yet compellingly of Jesus in her life. The contrasting styles of rhetoric helped to highlight their common message.

"It is amusing that what I always thought of as a Baptist style was used by Father Bertolucci. The calm rationality which I thought more representative of the Catholic was Mrs. Stapleton's. Thus my human classifications were thrown down by God doing for me a new thing."

Praising the Lord was a wonderful experience for Ann P. Petrino of New Rochelle, New York. Jesus 78 gave her a greater spiritual infilling and taught her to increase her giving of praise and thanks. In her words, "We should have more rallies giving thanks and praise to Jesus."

"Jesus 78 was a day I will long remember," professed

The People Are the Prophecy

Mrs. Ann E. Zelonis, a member of the Light of the World Prayer Group, Warminster, Pennsylvania. "It was great to see so many people of various churches and denominations coming together to praise the Lord. With His help, the unity He desires will soon be acclaimed. Am looking forward to Jesus 79."

Valerie Riggio, Linden, New Jersey, a member of the Immaculate Conception Prayer Group, and Trinity Assembly of God in Elizabeth, found Jesus 78 to be a tremendous blessing and witness to the power of God moving in the lives of people today. "It was a time of my recommitment and rededication to the Lord. I was touched deeply by the Spirit's flow of unity among all the Christians. It seemed to free me from the narrow minded 'my church is better than your church' merry-go-round.

"I saw my role as a Christian young person more clearly; that it is up to me and the rest of us, who profess to know and love the Lord Jesus Christ, to win this world for Christ by our own love. It has lived with me ever since. I am not the same person that I was before. My life has been opened to a new realization of the love, majesty and unconditional love of God."

Mrs. Miriam Hull, Rahway, New Jersey commented, "Even before accepting Jesus as my personal Savior and being baptized in the Holy Spirit, I had felt sad and frustrated by the division in Christianity, especially since much of the division has been caused by man-made doctrines and theology.

"At Jesus 78 the joy that filled my soul is indescribable. At different times and through the various speakers, my tears of joy were shed unashamedly. I praise the Lord for what He is doing on this earth today; also for being alive at this time."

A member of Our Lady of Mercy Convent, Port Chester, New York found Jesus 78 one of the greatest days in her life. Mrs. Lucille Acocella comments, "I wish I could live continually in the way I was lifted up all day long—have the same loving spirit, full confidence in the Lord and be able to share it with others. I look forward to attending more of the same in the future."

From Mrs. Joseph Troiano, Nutley, New Jersey came these words: "As long as I live, Jesus 78 will remain a most memorable day in my life. I pray that the faith and insight given to me that day will continue to make me grow in Jesus Christ. I am sure everyone who attended experienced the beautiful power of the Holy Spirit. I look forward to attending Jesus 79."

A baby in the Lord at age thirty-three, Mrs. Diane Gravenese of Norristown, Pennsylvania freely admitted that she had never raised her hands to praise the Lord. She reports, "I attended Jesus 78 with an open heart. I was totally unprepared for the strong, cold wind that day, having worn a thin windbreaker. To add to my discomfort, my jacket was accidentally ripped aboard the bus and was held together by two safety pins."

Mrs. Gravenese, a member of St. Helene's Church, sat with the Clairmonts, a couple who had been much inspiration to her in their "Life in the Spirit" seminar and who happened to have a large eight-by-ten piece of plastic with them. She explained, "I didn't want to freeze, so I sat among those 60,000 people wrapped up in this giant, dusty, stinky plastic. I started to thaw out a little as I listened to the talks. I saw the love and the power of the Spirit touch everyone in attendance. I thought how can you stand there looking like a giant, dusty Baggie trying to keep warm and not be embarrassed? Actually I was mortified.

"I lifted both arms to the sky and started to cry. Praise God! The plastic whipped off and surrounded the woman on my left. I recovered it to keep her from smothering and told her, 'I thought I would order it in pink.' We all smiled, forgot about the plastic and I've been praising the Lord ever since."

An interesting and inspiring letter came from Lee E. Elliott of Cumberland, Rhode Island. He's an analyst for the Allendale Insurance Company and a layperson in the Arnold Mills United Methodist Church. He brought a busload of thirty or more people to Jesus 78. The group assembled at 5:30 A.M. for the three-hour ride to the Meadowlands. They represented several different churches of various denominations in northern Rhode Island. Most of them had heard about the rally and the bus trip by word of mouth.

"Most were strangers to each other," Elliott commented, "but when they climbed aboard the bus we acted as a family within a few minutes. We recognized that we were all of one family—Christ's. Praise God!"

The group arrived late because a traffic accident in New York backed up traffic. Because of their late arrival, they were relegated to finding seats in the third tier of the stadium. "This would have caused a problem," Elliott explained, "had it not been for the video display units on the scoreboards at each end of the stadium. Through

193

these units we were able to participate in what was taking place down on the field.

"One very important part of the program for my group and me came in the words of prophecy delivered at various points throughout the day. They were meaningful to all of us. I also praise God for the speakers. Each of their messages was inspiring and open to the leading of the Holy Spirit. I could not recommend any greater gathering of charismatic leaders of today than those of Jesus 78.

"The highlight of the day for me personally came in the afternoon when everybody in the stadium participated in a litany of praise either through speaking in tongues or audible prayer. Praise God that I was able to participate in such a service and receive such a spirit of unbounded joy.

"On the return trip to Cumberland everyone had a difficult time returning to the commonplace. All had been filled to overflowing with the Holy Spirit and were in a state of joy and well-being. Each one had a different perspective of the meaningfulness of Jesus 78 and all began looking forward to Jesus 79, and vowing to bring another person with them."

CHAPTER 14

The Prophecy Revealed

Interdenominational neighborhood and home Bible study groups, involving prayer with Bible study, now are spreading throughout America and steadily increasing.

In line with the movement of God to unite the Body of Christ through Bible study and prayer, Mrs. Darlene Brown, Jackson, New Jersey wrote that "to confine a prayer meeting to a Catholic charismatic prayer meeting is like putting a lid on the Holy Spirit."

She was particularly burdened concerning the separation in the Communion of Catholics and Protestants. She cited the following Scripture verses bearing on Christ's desire for unity: Ephesians 2:2, 5, 13, 19 and 1 Corinthians 12:27-28.

Mrs. Brown commented, "If we as brothers and sisters proclaim the same Christ, why can we not break bread together? When Father Bertolucci spoke, I knew why the Lord wanted me at Jesus 78—to realize that others have the same burden. To God be the glory!" Mrs. Brown is a member of the Spirit of the Living God Prayer Group.

PROPHECY IN ACTION

Mrs. Nancy Gregory, a member of St. Timothy's Prayer Group in Philadelphia, reflected that a few months before Jesus 78, as she glanced up at her picture of the Sacred Heart of Jesus, He seemed to say, "My heart is broken." She stated, "I prayed for an answer to those words. The answer came the day of the rally. The program theme, 'That all may be one' and the words of previous prophecies, citing the disunity among the churches revealed to the world, 'The Body of my Son is broken.' The Lord will never cease to amaze me. That He could care so much for each of us, that He would speak to our hearts of His love—amazing."

Praise and more praise filled a bus to Jesus 78. "A seed was planted in our little prayer group to charter a bus to Jesus 78," reported Mrs. Robert Corbo of Elizabethtown, New Jersey, a member of St. Elizabeth's prayer group. "We wanted to show others the power and mighty workings of the Spirit. The bus was quite expensive and we needed thirty-five passengers to break even. Only eight in our group could come, so we planted 'seeds' in other prayer groups.

"There was an enthusiastic response to the idea but reservations were slow. We agreed in prayer and asked our heavenly Father to help us give glory to His Son by filling the bus." She went on to tell of God's wonderful work in answer to their prayers.

"He gathered thirty-seven people from ten different towns. Some drove two and a half hours to join the others in a three-hour trip to the Meadowlands. They found that the more they praised God, the faster reservations came in. "Praising Him allowed us to see His power and participate in it. God likes suspenseful endings. The bus wasn't filled until the last week except for one seat. Three others wanted to come but couldn't."

"And it shall come to pass in the last days, saith God, I will pour out of my Spirit upon all flesh; and your sons and your daughters shall prophesy" (Acts 2:17). Several of those attending Jesus 78 wrote of prophecies and visions being fulfilled and revealed to them. "When I was baptized with the Holy Spirit, October 31, 1962, the Lord gave me a vision of Him sitting on a throne with throngs of people of all races around Him, hands uplifted, singing His praises," wrote Iris R. Jacobson, a member of the First Baptist Church, Kingston, New York.

She explained that the scene was so beautiful and joyful that she began laughing. "I have had no control over the laughter," she continued. "It came from deep within. Later I found that it was laughter in the Holy Spirit. Since that time it has been an earnest desire of my heart that God's people be united as one and that prejudices of doctrine and tradition be overcome.

"Two weeks before Jesus 78, the Lord kept giving me the Scripture John 17:21-26. I was really blessed when I found that the Scripture given at Jesus 78 was John 17:21 and the main theme was that of God's people being one. Being in the midst of all those people having different religious backgrounds and of various ethnic groups but with their hands uplifted in praise, made the vision I had seen become a reality. Praise God for His love."

Thelma A. Brown, West Lebanon, New Hampshire reported that while Jim Bakker was preaching about Jesus coming very soon, she was watching him very attentively. "Suddenly I did not see him. Instead I was looking at a fig tree, ripe with beautiful green leaves. It was in the midst of sunshine," Mrs. Brown explained. "Through the Spirit Jesus let me know it was a fig tree. I had never seen one before. I believe I had been somewhat slain in the Spirit.

"Later I checked in my Bible at Matthew 24:32-35 and read, 'From the fig tree learn its lesson: as soon as its branch becomes tender and puts forth its leaves, you know that summer is near. So also, when you see all these things, you know that he is near, at the very gates. Truly, I say to you, this generation will not pass away till all these things take place. Heaven and earth will pass away, but my words will not pass away'" (RSV). Mrs. Brown is a member of My Redeemer Praise and Prayer Group, Holy Redeemer Parish.

When Kathy Muscara of Yonkers, New York started to write her reflections on Jesus 78 the Lord gave her a prophecy containing an urgent appeal and a warning. It is as follows:

"The message is clear. The time is at hand. We the Lord's chosen, are to unite in Spirit. We, the Body, must be strengthened by oneness in each other and in Him. Our love for one another and the way we care for our family, must not consist of outward appearance, but of a deep love that is so strong it is incomprehensible, as is the Lord's love for us.

"Then, in our unity, we must go forth beyond all walls, deep waters, mountains and deserts. Before the Perfect One comes, it is the duty of the Body to go forth and gather the lost lambs. The Lord cannot collect His chosen from the four corners of the winds until *all* the chosen are prepared.

"Look around you with open eyes, you of the Lord's house. See that everywhere you look and wherever you listen, the Lord whispers, shouts, begs and acknowledges that we must unite. It is time for the walls between God's people to be destroyed. Saints everywhere hold spiritual hands unto Him. Forget vital differences for you are one in Him. Melt—you cold hearts. Prepare yourselves, for the hours grow short and the Lord is in need of His army to march forth into the land and possess it. The Lord is urging us. He is crying out to us. This is the time. It cannot wait a moment longer.

"I need you to love. You must go forth now, in my love. Through you, the world sees me. You are my feet through the world, bringing my love to a dying, starving earth. I weep, for I desire that no man perish but that all would listen and follow. It is by you that they have ears to hear. It is by you that my light can shine forth. Go! Join with all my children and make yourselves right before me. Give your iniquities to me and I will take them from you.

"When will you trust me? When will you allow me to water your faith that it may grow and you may go into the world and perform my works? How long will you refuse to yield yourselves totally to me? I know what you hold on to, and I say to you, let go. Those things you love that are not of me, cast them aside.

"My anger will grow fierce and I will not withhold my punishments to my children. For, as your Father, I cannot tolerate your disobedience. Behold, my love is far greater than my anger. I say to you now is the time to put all things aside for me, for I am the Lord and I have spoken it. Go forth with love, my children. Lift me up. Yes, lift me up and I will draw all men unto me." Kathy Muscara is a member of the Pinecrest Retreat Centers, Setauket, New York.

Mrs. Joseph B. Conolly, Jr. of Glen Head, New York reported that she was thinking that Jesus 78 was not too special—"a little old hat," as she expressed it. But then, "Wham! Suddenly I fell into a deep meditation and an awareness of the presence of God as I've never had before. God is present in everything, every atom of the air, grass, the living people and even the concrete of the stadium. But not only there but in the whole world, every atom contains God Himself. I left Meadowlands with a new love and respect for everyone and everything in the whole world."

Mark 16:17 promises, "And these signs shall follow them that believe; In my name shall they cast out devils; they shall speak with new tongues."

Several attending Jesus 78 reported receiving the gift of tongues as part of their experience that day. Richard Eggens, Stony Point, New York, a leader in the Paraclete Community, wrote: "I brought my seven-year-old son with me to Jesus 78. At the conclusion of the day, when we were praising the Lord and agreeing on unity in the Body of Christ, I was praying out loud in tongues. Suddenly I was stunned to hear my son speaking in a strange language. I questioned Jesus at that moment and received instant peace in the words, 'Let the little ones come unto me.' Since then my son and I talk constantly about Jesus and he wants to come to my Friday night prayer meeting."

Another experience is related by Mrs. Florence Gannon of Purdy, New York, a member of St. Joseph's Prayer Community. She wrote, "All in our group were overwhelmed by the large number of people attending Jesus 78 raising their arms in praise to the Lord. On the way home in the bus, a young girl, seventeen years old, received the gift of tongues. Since then she has come to love Jesus and rely on Him for all her needs."

Attending Jesus 78 resulted in Jeanette Kurtz, Parksville, New York, receiving the gift of tongues. She reported, "It is a power I can't express in words." She belongs to the Liberty, New York Prayer Group.

Carol Hartung, East Greenwich, Rhode Island was impressed with the unfolding of prophecies at Jesus 78. She wrote: "Looking down from the high balcony of the stadium and watching the unfolding of prophecies I had heard at Jerusalem and Kansas City was the greatest experience of my life. I had been in Jerusalem at the Holy Spirit Conference in 1977 where I first heard the words, 'the healing of the broken Body of Christ,' from the speakers Father Francis Martin and David du Plessis. It struck me very hard. Later, some of us were in the Upper Room with Christians of many different denominations. We prayed that, starting in the Upper Room, we would be part of the healing of Christ's broken Body. Jesus said at the Last Supper that He would send His Holy Spirit to us. After He rose the Holy Spirit fell on the disciples at Pentecost.

"At Kansas City the same words came again. 'Weep and mourn, for the Body of my Son is broken. Heal my broken

Body.'

"To be at Jesus 78 with 60,000 or more Christians of various denominations, and to hear Father Bertolucci say the same thing with the scoreboards echoing the words and all the people standing and agreeing was tremendous. Then, at the same time, to see the sun break through and a white bird fly around the stadium, I felt there was a great magnet in the sky, and that we might be *raptured* en masse. Truly God is working out His will."

First Corinthians 12:25-26 warns, "There should be no schism in the body; but that the members should have the same care one for another. And whether one member suffer, all the members suffer with it; or one member be honored, all the members rejoice with it."

The above Scripture was pertinent to Mrs. Beth Frazer at Jesus 78. She reported, "While Andrae Crouch was singing we were to look up toward heaven at a certain part. I had just taken a drink of water when the moment arrived. As I raised my head, I choked. I have choked many times before but, believe me, nothing like this. I could not breathe or swallow or even cough.

"I flew out of my seat and stood on the steps, my daughter at my side. I remember thinking, 'So this is it, Lord. Graduation day, as Harold Hill says. I'm coming home today.' I felt no pain, no fear, just no breath. I was at peace.

"After what seemed like an eternity, and I felt that everything was beginning to leave my body, my daughter gave me a cup of water and said, 'Take one sip.' When I did everything was released. I know that Jesus touched me right then. Later I learned that the wonderful brothers and sisters in the Lord all around had held out hands in love and prayers toward me. How great is Jesus!"

Mrs. Frazer is a member of the Alleluia Prayer Group, St. Francis Church, Gettysburg, Pennsylvania. She also attends the New Jerusalem Prayer Group, St. Joseph's Provincial House, Emmettsburg, Maryland.

Unbounded joy, especially during a time of singing, deep prayer and praise characterizes the sentiment expressed in the following letters. Great spiritual unity and power prevailed. When the clouds parted and the sun shone through, during prayer, it was like a special response from God.

Mary Ann Nagle, member of a prayer group in Tarrytown, New York, captured the moment on film. She related, "The power of God was electrifying as evidenced by the tear-stained faces all around. I looked up and saw a cross emerging as light in the gray sky. I had a camera and my friend motioned for me to take a picture.

"The face of Jesus is faintly implanted in the center of the Cross. Above the Cross, the Father is seen seemingly blowing His Spirit into us. The Star of David is at the right and left of the Cross.

"This picture is wordless testimony of the nearness of Jesus and His coming. The hunger in our hearts for Jesus and the Holy Spirit is overwhelming. To reach up into the open sky while praising His Holy Name was a pleasure beyond words."

From Mrs. Charles (Patricia) Legge, a member of the Prayer and Praise Group in the Methodist Church in Haddonfield, New Jersey, came these words. "Jesus 78 was one of the most fantastic moments in my walk with the Lord. As our bus approached the stadium, everyone we passed was singing and waving greetings to each other. A feeling of fellowship and warmth surged through my veins. As we sang and listened to the teachings inspired by the Holy Spirit, my joy increased. When the clouds parted and the sun shone through, His radiant presence was felt by all."

Norma E. Camacho expressed confidence in the presence of the Lord throughout the day. A member of the New Commandment Prayer Group in Philadelphia, Pennsylvania, she wrote: "I felt so filled with the Holy Spirit that I couldn't help smiling. Some of my brothers and sisters in the Lord saw a white dove circling the stadium during the entire rally. I didn't see it but many did. It must mean something special. I know it did to many, including myself, when I was told about it. The Lord is always with us, filling us with His love and Spirit. Praise you, Jesus, You are Lord of lords."

An experience related by Esther Braglia of St. Hugh's Catholic Church in Huntington, New York, told what she felt when Father Bertolucci asked the audience to stand, raise their hands to the Lord and pray for the "Holy Spirit to come down upon us." Mrs. Braglia reported, "I felt His presence so strongly that I commenced to smile with tears rolling down my face. I asked Jesus to give us a sign that He was present. At that very moment, on that windy, overcast day, the sun 'Son' shone through. Praise God! Jesus Christ, our Lord, was there."

A similar type experience was sent in by Mrs. Martin Kolano, Passaic, New Jersey. "As we were singing, following the prayer for the Holy Spirit to join us, the tears began to roll down. The sun shining through was a beautiful sign to let us know the Holy Spirit came."

A member of the Mennonite Church, Levittown, Pennsylvania, Doris Denno, related the following: "Jesus 78 was such an awe-inspiring experience that I had trouble telling people about it. The presence of the Holy Spirit was so sweet and powerful that it couldn't be expressed in mere words. When the sun came through the clouds, it was as if God reached down and touched each one with His love."

The experience of several at Jesus 78 revealed the Lord's watchful eye over the movements of His people and His perfect timing in bringing them together. One such experience was related by Van B. Bruner, Jr. of Haddonfield, New Jersey. He reported, "Many years ago I joined an architectural firm and worked with Eric Chung, a Chinese draftsman. We became good friends but at the time neither of us was born again.

"As my wife and I were leaving the stadium, Eric and his wife walked right into our pathway. For the first time in many years we saw each other. We embraced and shared Jesus Christ in our lives. God ordained that meeting out of the some 60,000 attending. It truly was a miracle."

A somewhat opposite type of meeting was the experience of Jack M. Jonza and family of Vernon, New York, members of the Love and Joy of Jesus Prayer Group in the Church of the Holy Family. Jack relates: "Bob and Claire Vollmer, members of our prayer group, had gone on a southerly vacation with their family. They said that they might stop at Jesus 78 on their way. My family and I left the night before the rally and stopped at a motel nearby in New Jersey. Saturday morning we left for the Meadowlands and followed the throngs in. We went higher and higher looking for seats and a good vantage point. Finally in the upper mezzanine we found six chair seats. We took off our coats to settle down. I turned around and, behold, the Vollmers, with their four girls, were in the row behind us. Prasie the Lord! Twelve people out of more than 60,000."

A somewhat similar but yet different experience was encountered by Susan Ascolese of the Calvary Temple in Brooklyn in the search she and her husband had in obtaining seats. She stated, "Our church buses were leaving too early for us, so we decided to go by ourselves. Inside the stadium my husband stopped at an aisle and said, 'Let's find a seat here.' I said that I preferred to go to another section. We agreed on another spot and got an usher to seat us. Once seated, we began to see familiar faces. We were sitting with a church group we knew. God put us where we belonged."

Some young people came directly from their Senior Proms to Jesus 78. Maureen Colgan of Lansdowne, Pennsylvania wrote, "I was really confused whether to go or not. The night before was my Senior Prom. But I really had a desire to go. We gave our names to our leader and knew that it all was in God's hands. We went right from the prom. It was a beautiful experience. Even though it was cold, one could feel the warmth of God. The people were so wonderful."

Bernard F. Simon of Baltimore, Maryland wrote that he was pleased to find a special section reserved for the deaf. "It was a great joy to meet and renew acquaintances with the deaf and interpreters from other cities. Most of them I had not seen since the conference in Atlantic City in 1977."

Dorothea McGee of Lodi, New Jersey was interviewed by WCBS-TV. She's a member of St. Francis De Sales Prayer Group. She was surprised that everything in the interview was omitted except her reference to the number of fellow-believers present. "They did put me on the news," she wrote. "The Holy Spirit thus pushed me into witnessing when asked about my TV experience by around fifty people who otherwise would have resented my mentioning it."

Sister Julia Jamink, a member of the Sister of Charity, served on the planning committee for the Jesus 78 rally in Giants' Stadium. A member of the People of HOPE, she serves as administrator of HOPE's charismatic renewal center.

HOPE is a community dedicated to prayer and evangelization, and Sister Julia points out that the world today hungers to know that Jesus is alive and real and in our midst. She is convinced that the world needs to hear that Jesus is alive and real from the people who believe it in the depths of their own hearts. The world needs a witnessing from the community of believers.

"To evangelize," says Sister Julia, "is to proclaim Jesus, to proclaim in love, to proclaim in truth."

Sister Julia quotes from Pope Paul VI who said of evangelization in the modern world, "Those who seriously accept the Good News . . . gather together in Jesus' name in order to seek together the Kingdom, build it up and live in it. They make up a community which is in its turn evangelizing. . . ."

Sister Julia is certain that the result of evangelization is a changed heart, a changed heart which comes from committing one's life to Jesus under the power of the Holy Spirit.

Looking Ahead

The seed planted in the Meadowlands is beginning to sprout. Information requests for Jesus 79 are being received at both the People of HOPE and Logos. A national planning committee composed of leadership representing national and international charismatic ministers is in the formative stage. Regional leadership is emerging and overseas interest is mounting.

The success of the Jesus 78 Rally has been widely proclaimed around the world. People are talking in many languages in many nations about the miracles at Jesus 78. The greatest miracle was how the Holy Spirit drew together in love Christians from all historic church backgrounds and races. If it can happen along America's eastern seaboard, it can happen anywhere in the world. Why? Because the area from which the Jesus 78 Rally at Giants' Stadium drew its attendance is a population of all races, colors and creeds.

It was hard for the cynics to believe it could happen. It was even more difficult for them to understand why it did happen. But the Holy Spirit was present that day on the eve of Pentecost Sunday. The name of Jesus Christ was the magnet that drew in love so great that His love flowed into the hearts of more than 60,000 people and emanated from them with a love and compassion for each other. No one in the stadium will ever forget witnessing more than 60,000 people standing with their arms on the shoulders of each person on either side of them and swaying in unison from left to right as they sang hymns and praised the Lord. It was like watching some giant machine in rhythmic motion—securely anchored into position and yet its upper part swaying from left to right and back again.

The emotion-charged atmosphere became contagious. People cried. Others laughed joyously. Some praised the Lord. Others uttered silent prayers. There were the unsaved suddenly giving their hearts to Jesus Christ. There were healings of the body and of broken families. One woman who had found it difficult to walk up the steps in a tier to her seat because of braces on her legs, left after one of the messages and returned later without the braces. Around her arose a great commotion as those with her began gathering about her and praising the Lord for her healing.

Another woman, Mrs. Alberta Kelly of Cornwells Heights, Pennsylvania, fell and injured her ankle. She could not put her weight on it. But after a prayer the pain subsided and she was able to walk normally. Many others had personal encounters with Jesus Christ and a deeper devotion to the Holy Spirit. The list of miracles could continue endlessly as reported by those experiencing them.

Father Ferry reported on Jesus 78 at the recent International Catholic Charismatic Conference in Dublin, Ireland:

> "To evangelize today is to bring the good news to a world immersed in bad news," said the priest, "to counter the world's 'achievement' stance with a 'faith' stance." He shared about the success of the recent Jesus 78 rally, which brought together 55,000 Christians, Catholic and Protestant, in an ecumenical gathering at Giants' Stadium in New Jersey. "I come before you as a dreamer," explained Ferry, who hopes that the scene will be repeated next year at Pentecost, but on an even larger scale in cities and stadiums throughout the world.
>
> (*New Covenant*, Sept. 1978)

The one clarion call to come out of Jesus 78 was that the unity found there in the Body of Christ must continue, not only through 1979 but until Jesus Christ returns to set up His kingdom. It will continue as Jesus rallies are staged in such major cities as Boston, Philadelphia, Atlanta, Chicago, Los Angeles, San Francisco; Warsaw, Poland; Seoul, South Korea; and Munich, West Germany. There is no city or community in the world which cannot sponsor a Jesus rally through prayer and dedicated workers cooperating with the leadership now forming to sponsor such rallies.

Can you imagine one million Christians, or even more, assembled together around the world on the same day from every kindred and tribe and all singing simultaneously,

All hail the power of Jesus' Name!
Let angels prostrate fall;
Bring forth the royal diadem,
And crown Him Lord of all.

The experience at Jesus 78 in Giants' Stadium in the Meadowlands Sports Complex has set the stage. It proved it can happen. Jesus doesn't want His Body broken. He wants His Body healed and restored. He wants us all to be one in Him. His prayer is being answered.

For free information on how to receive
the international magazine

LOGOS JOURNAL

also Book Catalog

Write: Information - LOGOS JOURNAL CATALOG
Box 191
Plainfield, NJ 07061

Epilogue

Jesus 79 stadium meetings will be held in cities throughout the United States.

For information on the New York City meeting, write:

Dan Malachuk
Logos International
201 Church Street
Plainfield, N.J. 07060

Information on the New Jersey meeting may be obtained from:

Fr. Jim Ferry
People of HOPE
Xavier Center
Convent Station, N.J. 07961

In other cities, write:

CRS
237 North Michigan Street
South Bend, Indiana 46601